THE NEW HISTORY

THE WALDEN REPRINTS IN AMERICAN HISTORY

Lorenzo Sabine:
A Historical Essay on the Loyalists of the American Revolution

James Morton Callahan:
The Diplomatic History of the Southern Confederacy

James Harvey Robinson:
The New History

THE NEW HISTORY

Essays Illustrating The Modern Historical Outlook

By

JAMES HARVEY ROBINSON

With A Foreword

By

BENJAMIN KEEN

THE WALDEN PRESS

SPRINGFIELD, MASSACHUSETTS

1 9 5 8

Lithoprinted in U.S.A.
EDWARDS BROTHERS, INC.
Ann Arbor, Michigan

EDITOR'S FOREWORD

The essays composing this book first appeared as addresses and magazine articles between 1900 and 1912, a period of sharp controversy between historical conservatives and radicals in the United States. These radicals, who included James Harvey Robinson (1863-1936), Carl Becker, Charles Beard, and Lynn Thorndike, challenged the basic premises of the ruling "scientific" school of history: its devotion to "facts," its ideal of perfect objectivity, and its enthronement of political history as the leading thread in the historical process. They not only proposed to broaden the scope of history to include all social and intellectual developments, and to enlist all other sciences in the service of the historian, but they advanced a relativist and functional conception of history as an instrument used by groups to justify themselves in their own eyes and those of other men—a conception utterly alien to the "scientific" ideal of impersonal objectivity.

The New History, first published in 1912, presents in most readable form the guiding ideas of these rebels against historical orthodoxy. Robinson's simple and lively style, his capacity for cogent argument reinforced by a wealth of historical examples, and his infectious enthusiasm, gave his book a wide popularity and influence. By the early 1920's the heretics had won the day. The right of historians to explore the past from the economic, intellectual, or any other point of view that might prove illuminating had become firmly established (at least in theory). And by the mid-thirties relativism, as formulated by the later Becker and Beard, had become the fashionable creed of the historical guild in the United States.

Robinson's historical interpretation, it is important to note, differs markedly from that of the later Becker and Beard. The viewpoint of *The New History* is fundamentally evolutionary, rationalist, and optimistic. For Robinson the past is knowable. The historical knowledge and accounts of any generation are partial, defective, one-sided; but they contain a portion of truth which future generations of historians will enlarge and refine. Progressive social change or betterment is the law of history. The historian can help to establish the direction of change by the study of its roots in the past, and should teach men to cooperate with and control the forces of change in a process of conscious social readjustment.

In the hands of Becker and Beard, on the other hand, the relativist and functional conception of history developed into a skepticism that raised serious doubts as to the knowability of history and even reduced written history to an act of faith, thus excluding the possibility of fixing any pattern or direction in history or of controlling the process of change. In recent years this sterile skepticism has come under increasing attack (see, for example, Perez Zagorin's stimulating article, "Carl Becker on History," in the October, 1956 issue of the *American Historical Review*). In connection with the search for philosophical alternatives to the blind alley of relativism, a fresh look by historians at Robinson's theoretical position, with a view to determining its sound and unsound elements, may be in order. Certainly Robinson's emphasis on the social responsibility of history, and particularly his stress on the duty of the historian to promote receptivity to change, acceptance of the need for conscious social readjustment, could not be more timely than in our own day of immensely accelerated and explosive change.

For the rest, *The New History* continues to have great instructional value. The historical novice will find particular pleasure and profit in such charmingly written and thoughtful introductions to key themes as "The History of History," "The New Allies of History," and "Reflections on Intellectual History."

BENJAMIN KEEN

PREFACE

ALL of the essays in this volume, with the exception of the fourth, have been printed before, as addresses or contributions to periodicals. They have, however, not only been carefully revised, but have been adjusted so as to give as much coherence as possible to the collection. They all illustrate, each in its particular way, the conception of "the new history" developed in the first essay.

In No. I, I borrow portions from an article on "Popular Histories and their Defects" which appeared in the now defunct *International Monthly*, July, 1900, but have made a new use of them. The second paper was originally prepared as one in a series of non-technical lectures delivered at Columbia University in 1908 and published by the Columbia University Press. With it has been combined portions from a paper on "The New History" read before the Philosophical Society in Philadelphia, April 22, 1911. No. III was read before the American Historical Association, December, 1910, and printed in the *Journal of Philosophy, Psychology, and Scientific Method*, March 16, 1911, where No. VIII also appeared on May 11 of the same year.

No. V was read, under the caption "The Significance of History in Industrial Education," before the superintendents of the larger cities at the meeting of the National Educational Association at Indianapolis, March 2, 1910, and was printed in *The Educational Bi-Monthly*, June, 1910. No. VI was read before the New England Teachers Association at Hartford, April 27, 1906. No. VII is a combination of two articles: "The Tennis Court Oath," prepared for the meeting of the American Historical Association in 1894 and published in their proceedings and in the *Political Science Quarterly*, Vol. X, No. 3, and "The French Declaration of the Rights of Man," which was printed in the latter journal, Vol. XIV, No. 4; together with borrowings from an article in the *American Historical Review*, April, 1906, on "Some Recent Tendencies in the Study of the French Revolution."

J. H. R.

COLUMBIA UNIVERSITY, NEW YORK,
November, 1911.

TABLE OF CONTENTS

THE NEW HISTORY

In its amplest meaning History includes every trace and vestige of everything that man has done or thought since first he appeared on the earth. It may aspire to follow the fate of nations or it may depict the habits and emotions of the most obscure individual. Its sources of information extend from the rude flint hatchets of Chelles to this morning's newspaper. It is the vague and comprehensive science of past human affairs. We are within its bounds whether we decipher a mortgage on an Assyrian tile, estimate the value of the Diamond Necklace, or describe the over-short pastry to which Charles V was addicted to his undoing. The tragic reflections of Eli's daughter-in-law, when she learned of the discomfiture of her people at Ebenezer, are history; so are the provisions of Magna Charta, the origin of the doctrine of transubstantiation, the fall of Santiago, the difference between a black friar and a white friar, and the certified circulation of the *New York World* upon February 1 of the current year. Each fact has its interest and importance; all have been carefully recorded.

Now, when a writer opens and begins to peruse the thick, closely written volume of human experience,

B   1

with a view of making an abstract of it for those who have no time to study the original work, he is immediately forced to ask himself what he shall select to present to his readers' attention. He finds that the great book from which he gains his information is grotesquely out of perspective, for it was compiled by many different hands, and by those widely separated in time and in sentiment — by Herodotus, Machiavelli, Eusebius, St. Simon, Otto of Freising, Pepys, St. Luke, the Duchess of Abrantès, Sallust, Cotton Mather. The portentously serious alternates with the lightest gossip. A dissipated courtier may be allotted a chapter and the destruction of a race be left unrecorded. It is clear that in treating history for the general reader the question of selection and proportion is momentous. Yet when we turn to our more popular treatises on the subject, the obvious and pressing need of picking and choosing, of selecting, reselecting, and selecting again, would seem to have escaped most writers. They appear to be the victims of tradition in dealing with the past. They exhibit but little appreciation of the vast resources upon which they might draw, and unconsciously follow, for the most part, an established routine in their selection of facts. When we consider the vast range of human interests, our histories furnish us with a sadly inadequate and misleading review of the past, and it might almost seem as if historians had joined in a conspiracy to foster a narrow and relatively unedi-

fying conception of the true scope and intent of historical study. This is apparent if we examine any of
the older standard outlines or handbooks from which
a great part of the public has derived its notions of
the past, either in school or later in life.

The following is an extract from a compendium
much used until recently in schools and colleges:
"Robert the Wise (of Anjou) (1309–1343), the successor of Charles II of Naples, and the champion of
the Guelphs, could not extend his power over Sicily
where Frederick II (1296–1337), the son of Peter of
Aragon, reigned. Robert's granddaughter, Joan I,
after a career of crime and misfortune, was strangled
in prison by Charles Durazzo, the last male descendant
of the house of Anjou in Lower Italy (1382), who
seized on the government. Joan II, the last heir of
Durazzo (1414–1435), first adopted Alfonso V, of
Aragon, and then Louis III, of Anjou, and his brother,
René. Alfonso, who inherited the crown of Sicily,
united both kingdoms (1435), after a war with René
and the Visconti of Milan."

This is not, as we might be tempted to suspect, a
mere collection of data for contingent reference, no
more intended to be read than a table of logarithms.
It is a characteristic passage from the six pages which
a distinguished scholar devotes to the Italy of Dante,
Petrarch, and Lorenzo the Magnificent. In preparing a guide for more advanced pupils and the
general reader, the author's purpose was, he tells us,

"that it should present the essential facts of history in due order, . . . that it should point out clearly
the connection of events and of successive eras with one
another; that through the interest awakened by the
natural, unforced view gained of this unity of history
and by such illustrative incidents as the brevity of the
narrative would allow to be wrought into it, the dryness of a mere summary should be so far as possible
relieved." Now, in treating the Italian Renaissance, this writer has chosen barely to mention the
name of Francesco Petrarca, but devotes a twelfth
of the available space to the interminable dynastic
squabbles of southern Italy. We may assume that
this illustrates his conception of "the essential facts
of history presented in due order," for the extracts
quoted above can hardly be an example of "illustrative incidents" wrought in to relieve the dryness of a
mere summary.

I open a more recent volume which treats of the
whole of Europe in the eighteenth century, as it
approached the momentous crisis of the French Revolution. Its author could hardly fail to realize the
necessity of sifting his material most critically in
order to make clear the regenerative workings of the
new spirit of enlightenment amid conditions essentially
difficult for us to understand. He does not hesitate,
however, to insert such statements as these: "Zinzendorf died in 1742, Stahremberg in 1745, Kinsky in
1748. While Uhlfeld became on Zinzendorf's death

nominally chancellor, Bartenstein remained from 1740 to 1753 Minister of Foreign Affairs, and had the greatest influence in the secret conference of Ministers." Very true; but were there not, perhaps, other things better worth telling about an ill-understood century than the dates of the deaths of the members of an Austrian cabinet?

An able historian of the French Revolution, who finds no time to tell us how it all came about, cheerfully devotes many paragraphs to matters like the following: "The bailliage of Aunis claimed to be independent of Saintonge, the royal bailliage of Nivernais asserted that it included the ducal bailliage, and the old quarrel between Upper and Lower Auvergne again broke out. Similar rivalry appeared between the cities of Riom and Clermont-Ferrand, each claiming to be the capital of the bailliage of Lower Auvergne, and between the towns of Clermont-en-Argonne and Varennes; Chateauneuf-en-Thimerais asserted that it was a royal bailliage, and not dependent on Chartres."

The tendency to catalogue mere names of persons and places which have not the least importance for the reader, or which for want of space must be left as undetermined as x, y, and z in an unsolved equation, is too common to require further illustration. The question forces itself upon us, why do writers include such seemingly irrelevant and unedifying details? Sometimes, doubtless, from mere thoughtlessness;

the names mean something to the writer, who mistakenly infers that they are eloquent in themselves. Or he may suppose that they give greater vivacity to his tale, or will form the nucleus about which future knowledge may crystallize. Names but once mentioned, however, rarely add vividness to a story, but rather obscure it ; and it is safe to say that the mention of Durazzo, Clermont-Ferrand, Kinsky, and René are little likely to stimulate farther historical research, but rather to promote general obfuscation.

It is, however, often urged that even the hastiest and driest chronicle of the "chief events" in the world's history is a good thing, — that we get at least a chronological outline which we carry about with us as a guide, which enables us to put our future knowledge in its proper relations. We learn important dates so as to read intelligently later of events of which in school we learn only the names. We prepare ourselves to place our contingent knowledge of literature, philosophy, institutions, and art in what is called an "historic setting." Many of us have, however, come to suspect that such an outline amounts to very little. It recommends itself, it is true, as the easiest kind of history to teach, since it requires no thought, — only memory. I once had occasion to ask a college professor of great erudition and culture, who had resided several years in the Orient, the date of the Hegira, which, with that of Marathon, and the battle of Crécy, is generally regarded as part of the equipment of every

educated gentleman. He did not know the date,
however, any better than I did, so we looked it up
in a dictionary. We might, indeed, have saved a
minute or two if we had had the information at our
tongue's end, but we had never missed it before.

A sensible carpenter or plumber does not constantly
carry a saw in his hip pocket, or a coil of lead pipe
over his shoulder, in order to be ready for a distant
emergency. He very properly goes to his shop and
his tool chest for his tools and materials. No more,
in these days of cheap and convenient books of reference, need the student of history go heavy-armed
for intellectual encounters. Of course all knowledge,
even that which is well forgotten, may beget a certain
habit of accuracy and sense of proportion, but formulas should follow knowledge, as they do in our best
mathematical textbooks; in historical instruction we
have ordinarily given our formulas first.

The really fundamental reason for hastening to
introduce the reader as early as possible to the son of
Peter of Aragon, to Zinzendorf, and that historic
spot, Chateauneuf-en-Thimerais, has doubtless been
the venerable predilection for merely political events
and persons which has until recently dominated our
writers of popular history. Carlyle's warning has
passed unheeded, that far away from senate houses,
battle fields, and king's antechambers, "the mighty
tide of thought and action was still rolling on its
wondrous course." Elaborate attempts have indeed

been made to justify this seemingly disproportionate fondness for political and military affairs. We are bluntly told by Mr. Freeman that "History is past politics." To Ranke the purpose of history was to clarify our notions of the origin and nature of the State, which forms the basis of the continuity that we believe we observe in human development. Another German scholar claims that for thousands of years the State, the political organism, has been the chief and predominating theme of historical research and that it should remain so.[1]

It is impossible to discuss here the intricate question of the rôle of the State in the past; nor is it necessary to do so, for no one denies its great importance or would advocate its neglect in our historical manuals. The real question is, has not our bias for political history led us to include a great many trifling details of dynasties and military history which merely confound the reader and take up precious space that should be devoted to certain great issues hitherto neglected? The winning or losing of a bit of territory by a Louis or a Frederick, the laborious piecing together of a puny duchy destined to speedy disinte-

[1] A bitter war was waged for some years among German scholars over the question of the proper scope of history, whether the State or general culture is its proper theme. Professor Schmoller denounces the effort to assert the exclusive claims of political history as "jene Neigung enger bornierter Geister, die ihre Blössen mit Scheuklappen zudecken um einen Rechstitel fur ihre Unwissenheit auf den Nachbargebieten zu haben." *Jahrb. f. Gesetzgebung*, etc., Vol. XIII, p. 1484.

gration upon the downfall of a Cæsar Borgia, struggles between rival dynasties, the ambitions of young kings' uncles, the turning of an enemy's flank a thousand years ago, — have not such things been given an unmerited prominence? Man is more than a warrior, a subject, or a princely ruler; the State is by no means his sole interest. In the Middle Ages he organized a church more permanent, more penetratingly powerful, by all accounts, than any civil government ever seen, even that of Rome itself. He has, through the ages, made voyages, extended commerce, founded cities, established great universities, written books, built glorious cathedrals, painted pictures, and sought out many inventions. The propriety of including these human interests in our historical manuals is being more and more widely recognized, but political history still retains its supreme position, and past political events are still looked upon by the public as history *par excellence*.

In contrast, and even in seeming contradiction, to the tradition which gives prominence to political events and personages, there is a curious element of the sensational in our popular histories. There is a kind of history which does not concern itself with the normal conduct and serious achievements of mankind in the past, but, like melodrama, purposely selects the picturesque and lurid as its theme. The annals of France, a modern writer assures us, will always command special attention, for "No other

modern nation has undergone changes more frequent,
more radical, more sudden, bloody, and dramatic."
Then, too: "No land has given birth to men more
great, more good, more brave; none has been cursed
with men more vile. No people have climbed higher
in the arduous pathway of victory; none have been
so pitilessly stricken down in defeat." In short,
"France has furnished the epic poem of modern
history." The writer would therefore convince us
that the more prodigious the occurrences narrated,
the better the history. A distinguished chemist once
considerately told me that it seemed to him that the
certitude of history varied in inverse ratio to what
we know about it. He might have added that sometimes, in common with the *Police Gazette*, its intrin-
sic interest appears to vary in direct ratio to its grue-
someness.

There would be less objection to perpetuating the
conception of history as a chronicle of heroic persons
and romantic occurrences, were it not that the craving
for the dramatic can be better met by confessed fiction,
and that those who see in history an epic poem give
us very imperfect and erroneous notions of the past.
In no other subject of study except history, is fortuitous prominence accepted as a measure of importance.
The teacher of chemistry does not confine himself
to pretty experiments, but conscientiously chooses
those that are most typical and instructive. Metallic
potassium and liquefied air are less common in the

laboratory than water, lime, and sulphuric acid. What would be the opinion in regard to a clinical lecturer who dwelt upon leprosy and the bubonic plague for fear his students might be bored by a description of the symptoms of measles and typhoid? In every study except history the teacher seeks to make the important and normal clear at any cost. All his expedients are directed to that one end. The rule, not the exception, is his object.

It is noteworthy, too, that we generally recognize the misleading character of descriptions of contemporaneous conditions in which only the sensational events are narrated. Romantic marriages and tragic deaths; the doings of poisoners, adulterers, and lunatics; the cases of those who have swallowed needles to find them coming out at unexpected places years after; who have taken laudanum for paregoric, or been run over by beer wagons; even the fullest account of such matters furnishes, after all, but a partial picture of the life of a great city to-day. Yet in the history of France alluded to above, the description of the feudal system scarcely extends beyond dungeons,—"Oh how damp, dark, and cold!"—knee clamps and thumbscrews. The medieval church was, we might infer, little more than the clever device of evil men to gratify greed and lasciviousness, and abounded in "humbugs, frauds, and bogus miracles." To make true statements is not necessarily to tell the truth. We may, like the "yellow" journalist, narrate facts, but with such reckless disregard of perspective, and with such a consistent anxiety to startle the reader, that unvarnished fiction would be preferable. A writer who, instead of endeavoring to make plain the true greatness of the church, says, "Miraculous oil was common, portions of the true cross plentiful, and such objects as St. Anne's comb and the Virgin Mary's petticoat were accessible to the devout," is guilty of gross misrepresentation within the bounds of formal accuracy.

The partiality exhibited by our popular writers for certain classes of historical facts is obviously no proof that other and more pertinent facts should not be brought to the reader's attention. For it may be, as we have seen, either that events are narrated simply because they are pleasing, or dramatic, or highly exceptional; or that they are mentioned because it is deemed proper that an educated man should know that Philip Augustus became king in 1180, and that the Battle of the Boyne was fought in 1690. But a writer who is governed by these motives in his selection of material will naturally produce a book in which famous episodes and mildly diverting anecdotes are given a didactic seriousness by a proper admixture of dry, traditional information.

We are, further, ordinarily taught to view mankind as in a periodic state of turmoil. Historical writers do all they can, by studied neglect, to disguise the importance of the lucid intervals during which the greater part of human progress has taken place. They skip lightly from one commotion to another. They have not time to explain what the French Revolution was by rationally describing the *Ancien régime*, which can alone give it any meaning, but after the quotation from La Bruyère, regarding certain fierce animals, "black, livid, and burnt by the sun," and a repetition of that careless phrase, "After us, the deluge," they hasten on to the Reign of Terror as the be-all and end-all of the bloody affair. And in this way they make a second St. Bartholomew's of one of the grandest and, in its essential reforms, most peaceful of changes which ever overtook France or Europe. Obviously the real significance of a revolution is to be measured by the extent to which general conditions were changed and new things substituted for the old. The old must, therefore, be studied quite as carefully as the new — more carefully, indeed, since our sympathies are usually with the new, and our knowledge of the more recent is fuller than that of the more remote. Hence, we might far better busy ourselves with the reasons why arbitrary imprisonments, the guilds, the sale of offices, and so forth, were defended by many thoughtful, well-intentioned citizens than waste time in a gratuitous denunciation of them.

I know that at this point the perfectly natural objection may be raised, that while institutions and gradual developments may be very legitimate objects of study for those already trained in historical work,

they are not proper subjects for any one except a
university student or an occasional serious-minded
and long-suffering general reader. Only conspicuous
events and striking crises are, it is ordinarily assumed,
within the scope of natural human interest, and the
influence of the personal element must, it is urged,
be exaggerated, simply because the general trend of
development and progress offers nothing which the
mind can easily grasp. We therefore substitute for
the real historical continuity a factitious continuity
and string our narrative upon a line of kings — Magnus
VI (1263–1281), followed by Erick II (1281–1299),
followed by Hakon V (1299–1320), followed by Magnus VII (1320–1365). No one will deny, however,
that most of the names in even the best-known dynasties remain mere names; and even if we learn that
Emperor Rudolph II was a learned man and an
astrologer, and his contemporary, Henry III of
France, "a debauched weakling," this knowledge in no
way aids us in grasping the most fundamental and
valuable truth which the past has to teach us, that of
historical continuity.

Those therefore who would view with distrust any
attempt radically to alter our current methods of
presenting general history, would probably withdraw
their opposition to a change, if some scheme could be
devised by which conditions and institutions could be
made interesting and comprehensible, and a real continuity be substituted for the kingly *nexus* with which

we now bind the past together. Now I firmly believe
that "institutions" (which are after all only national
habits) can be made interesting. I use the word "institutions" in a very broad sense to include the ways
in which people have thought and acted in the past,
their tastes and their achievements in many fields
besides the political. Events are the more or less
clear expression of "institutions" in this sense, and the
events properly selected will serve to make the "institutions" clear.

Hitherto writers have been prone to deal with events
for their own sake; a deeper insight will surely lead us,
as time goes on, to reject the anomalous and seemingly
accidental occurrences and dwell rather upon those
which illustrate some profound historical truth. And
there is a very simple principle by which the relevant
and useful may be determined and the irrelevant rejected. Is the fact or occurrence one which will aid
the reader to grasp the meaning of any great period of
human development or the true nature of any momentous institution? It should then be cherished as a
precious means to an end, and the more engaging it is,
the better; its inherent interest will only facilitate
our work, not embarrass it. On the other hand, is
an event seemingly fortuitous, isolated, and anomalous, — like the story of Rienzi, the September massacres, or the murder of Marat? We should then hesitate to include it on its own merits, — at least in a
brief historical manual — for, interesting as it may be

as an heroic or terrible incident, it may mislead the reader and divert his attention from the prevailing interests, preoccupations and permanent achievements of the past.

If we have not been unfair in our review of the more striking peculiarities of popular historiography, we find them to be as follows : —

(1) A careless inclusion of mere names, which can scarcely have any meaning for the reader and which, instead of stimulating thought and interest, merely weigh down his spirit.

(2) A penchant more or less irresistible to recite political events to the exclusion of other matters often of far greater moment.

(3) The old habit of narrating extraordinary episodes, not because they illustrate the general trend of affairs or the prevailing conditions of a particular time, but simply because they are conspicuous in the annals of the past. This results in a ludicrous disregard of perspective which assigns more importance to a demented journalist like Marat than to so influential a writer as Erasmus.

II

The essay which immediately follows this will be devoted to a sketch of the history of history, and will explain more fully the development of the older ideals of historical composition. It will make clear that these

ideals have changed so much from time to time that it
is quite possible that an essentially new one may in
time prevail.   History is doubtless

> An orchard bearing several trees
> And fruits of different tastes.

It may please our fancy, gratify our serious or idle
curiosity, test our memories, and, as Bolingbroke says,
contribute to " a creditable kind of ignorance."   But
the one thing that it ought to do, and has not yet effec-
tively done, is to help us to understand ourselves and
our fellows and the problems and prospects of mankind.   It is this most significant form of history's
usefulness that has been most commonly neglected.

It is true that it has long been held that certain
lessons could be derived from the past, — precedents
for the statesman and the warrior, moral guidance and
consoling instances of providential interference for
the commonalty.   But there is a growing suspicion,
which has reached conviction in the minds of most
modern historians, that this type of usefulness is purely
illusory.   The present writer is anxious to avoid any
risk of being regarded as an advocate of these supposed advantages of historical study.   Their value
rests on the assumption that conditions remain sufficiently uniform to give precedents a perpetual value,
while, as a matter of fact, conditions, at least in our
own time, are so rapidly altering that for the most part
it would be dangerous indeed to attempt to apply

c

past experience to the solution of current problems. Moreover, we rarely have sufficient reliable information in regard to the supposed analogous situation in the past to enable us to apply it to present needs. Most of the appeals of inexpensive oratory to "what history teaches" belong to this class of assumed analogies which will not bear close scrutiny. When I speak of history enabling us to understand ourselves and the problems and prospects of mankind, I have something quite different in mind, which I will try to make plain by calling the reader's attention to the use that he makes of his own personal history.

We are almost entirely dependent upon our memory of our past thoughts and experiences for an understanding of the situation in which we find ourselves at any given moment. To take the nearest example, the reader will have to consult his own history to understand why his eyes are fixed upon this particular page. If he should fall into a sound sleep and be suddenly awakened, his memory might for the moment be paralyzed, and he would gaze in astonishment about the room, with no realization of his whereabouts. The fact that all the familiar objects about him presented themselves plainly to his view would not be sufficient to make him feel at home until his memory had come to his aid and enabled him to recall a certain portion of the past. The momentary suspension of memory's functions as one recovers from a fainting fit or emerges from the effects of an anæsthetic is sometimes so distressing as to amount to a sort of intellectual agony. In its normal state the mind selects automatically, from the almost infinite mass of memories, just those things in our past which make us feel at home in the present. It works so easily and efficiently that we are unconscious of what it is doing for us and of how dependent we are upon it. It supplies so promptly and so precisely what we need from the past in order to make the present intelligible that we are beguiled into the mistaken notion that the present is self-explanatory and quite able to take care of itself, and that the past is largely dead and irrelevant, except when we have to make a conscious effort to recall some elusive fact.

What we call history is not so different from our more intimate personal memories as at first sight it seems to be; for very many of the useful and essential elements in our recollections are not personal experiences at all, but include a multitude of things which we have been told or have read; and these play a very important part in our life. Should the reader of this page stop to reflect, he would perceive a long succession of historical antecedents leading up to his presence in a particular room, his ability to read the English language, his momentary freedom from pressing cares, and his inclination to center his attention upon a discussion of the nature and value of historical study. Were he not vaguely conscious of these historical antecedents, he would be in the bewildered condition spoken

of above. Some of the memories necessary to save
him from his bewilderment are parts of his own past
experience, but many of them belong to the realm of
history, namely, to what he has been told or what he
has read of the past.

I could have no hope that this line of argument
would make the slightest impression upon the reader,
were he confined either to the immediate impressions of
the moment, or to his personal experiences. It gives
one something of a shock, indeed, to consider what a
very small part of our guiding convictions are in any
way connected with our personal experience. The
date of our own birth is quite as strictly historical a
fact as that of Artaphernes or of Innocent III; we are
forced to a helpless reliance upon the evidence of
others for both events.

So it comes about that our personal recollections
insensibly merge into history in the ordinary sense of
the word. History, from this point of view, may be
regarded as an artificial extension and broadening of
our memories and may be used to overcome the natural
bewilderment of all unfamiliar situations. Could we
suddenly be endowed with a Godlike and exhaustive
knowledge of the whole history of mankind, far more
complete than the combined knowledge of all the histories ever written, we should gain forthwith a Godlike appreciation of the world in which we live, and a
Godlike insight into the evils which mankind now suf-
fers, as well as into the most promising methods for alle-

viating them, *not because the past would furnish precedents of conduct, but because our conduct would be based
upon a perfect comprehension of existing conditions
founded upon a perfect knowledge of the past.* As yet we
are not in a position to interrogate the past with a view
to gaining light on great social, political, economic,
religious, and educational questions in the manner in
which we settle the personal problems which face us —
for example, whether we should make such and such a
visit or investment, or read such and such a book, — by
unconsciously judging the situation in the light of our
recollections. Historians have not as yet set themselves to furnish us with what lies behind our great
contemporaneous task of human betterment. They
have hitherto had other notions of their functions, and
were they asked to furnish answers to the questions that
a person *au courant* with the problems of the day would
most naturally put to them, they would with one accord begin to make excuses. One would say that it
had long been recognized that it was the historian's
business to deal with kings, parliaments, constitutions,
wars, treaties, and territorial changes; another would
declare that recent history cannot be adequately
written and that, therefore, we can never hope to
bring the past into relation with the present, but must
always leave a fitting interval between ourselves and
the nearest point to which the historian should venture
to extend his researches; a third will urge that to have
a purpose in historical study is to endanger those prin-

ciples of objectivity upon which all sound and scientific research must be based. So it comes about that our books are like very bad memories which insist upon recalling facts that have no assignable relation to our needs, and this is the reason why the practical value of history has so long been obscured.

In order to make still clearer our dependence upon history in dealing with the present, let the reader remember that we owe most of our institutions to a rather remote past, which alone can explain their origin. The conditions which produced the Holy Roman Apostolic Church, trial by jury, the Privy Council, the degree of LL.D., the Book of Common Prayer, "the liberal arts," were very different from those that exist to-day. Contemporaneous religious, educational, and legal ideals are not the immediate product of existing circumstances, but were developed in great part during periods when man knew far less than he now does. Curiously enough our habits of thought change much more slowly than our environment and are usually far in arrears. Our respect for a given institution or social convention may be purely traditional and have little relation to its value, as judged by existing conditions. We are, therefore, in constant danger of viewing present problems with obsolete emotions and of attempting to settle them by obsolete reasoning. This is one of the chief reasons why we are never by any means perfectly adjusted to our environment.

Our notions of a church and its proper function in society, of a capitalist, of a liberal education, of paying taxes, of Sunday observance, of poverty, of war, are determined only to a slight extent by what is happening to-day. The belief on which I was reared, that God ordained the observance of Sunday from the clouds of Sinai, is an anachronism which could not spontaneously have developed in the United States in the nineteenth century; nevertheless, it still continues to influence the conduct of many persons. We pay our taxes as grudgingly as if they were still the extortions of feudal barons or absolute monarchs for their personal gratification, although they are now a contribution to our common expenses fixed by our own representatives. Few have outgrown the emotions connected with war at a time when personal prowess played a much greater part than the Steel Trust. Conservative college presidents still feel obliged to defend the "liberal arts" and the "humanities" without any very clear understanding of how the task came to be imposed upon them. To do justice to the anachronisms in conservative economic and legal reasoning would require a whole volume.

Society is to-day engaged in a tremendous and unprecedented effort to better itself in manifold ways. Never has our knowledge of the world and of man been so great as it now is; never before has there been so much general good will and so much intelligent social activity as now prevails. The part that each of us can play in forwarding some phase of this reform will depend upon our understanding of existing conditions and opinion, and these can only be explained, as has been shown, by following more or less carefully the processes that produced them. We must develop historical-mindedness upon a far more generous scale than hitherto, for this will add a still deficient element in our intellectual equipment and will promote rational progress as nothing else can do. The present has hitherto been the willing victim of the past; the time has now come when it should turn on the past and exploit it in the interests of advance.

The "New History" is escaping from the limitations formerly imposed upon the study of the past. It will come in time consciously to meet our daily needs; it will avail itself of all those discoveries that are being made about mankind by anthropologists, economists, psychologists, and sociologists — discoveries which during the past fifty years have served to revolutionize our ideas of the origin, progress, and prospects of our race. There is no branch of organic or inorganic science which has not undergone the most remarkable changes during the last half century, and many new branches of social science, even the names of which would have been unknown to historians in the middle of the nineteenth century, have been added to the long list. It is inevitable that history should be involved in this revolutionary process, but since it must be confessed that this necessity has escaped many contemporaneous writers, it is no wonder that the intelligent public continues to accept somewhat archaic ideas of the scope and character of history.

The title of this little volume has been chosen with the view of emphasizing the fact that history should not be regarded as a stationary subject which can only progress by refining its methods and accumulating, criticizing, and assimilating new material, but that it is bound to alter its ideals and aims with the general progress of society and of the social sciences, and that it should ultimately play an infinitely more important rôle in our intellectual life than it has hitherto done.

THE HISTORY OF HISTORY

"History" is so vague a term at best, and has during the past twenty-five hundred years undergone such considerable changes in character and purpose, that it is well for one to review its somewhat startling vicissitudes if he desires to understand the conflicting notions which prevail to-day in regard to the significance of the past and the proper way of dealing with it. When we look back over the history of history, from Hecatæus of Miletus and Herodotus to the freshest doctor's dissertation, we perceive that its point of view has never been a settled one; that it has been the victim at once of routine and of transient circumstances. Some of its former ambitions it has now been forced to surrender; it has been chastened by a growing consciousness of ignorance; but these humiliations have been far more than offset by the extraordinary extension of its domain, which has taken place very recently and almost insensibly. Half a century ago, man's past was supposed to include less than six thousand years; now the story is seen to stretch back hundreds of thousands of years. But it is not man alone that has a history, — animals, plants, rocks, stars, even atoms, have theirs as well. So the zoölogist, the botanist, the geologist, the astronomer, even the chemist have come to worship at History's shrine.

The growth of historical-mindedness is thus perhaps the chief intellectual trait of our age. It is deeply affecting not only the social sciences but our general conceptions of the whole organic and inorganic world. Yet in its beginnings history had no very serious aims. It was doubtless discovered, in the first instance, by the story-teller, and its purpose has usually been to tell a tale rather than to contribute to a well-considered body of scientific knowledge. Indeed we shall not be far astray, if we view history, as it has existed through the ages, and even down to our own day, as a branch of general literature, the object of which has been to present past events in an artistic manner, in order to gratify a natural curiosity in regard to the achievements and fate of conspicuous persons, the rise and decay of monarchies, and the signal commotions and disasters which have repeatedly afflicted humanity.

Although the persistence of this primitive notion of history is so obvious as scarcely to demand illustration, it is interesting to note that as late as 1820, Daunou, a reputable French historian of his time, in a course of lectures upon the pursuit of history delivered at the Collège de France, declares that the masterpieces of epic poetry should claim the first attention of the would-be historian, since it is the poets who have created the art of narrative. Then, from the modern novel, Daunou continues, the student may learn "the method of giving an artistic pose to persons and events, of distributing details, of skillfully carrying on the thread of the narrative, of interrupting it, of resuming it, of sustaining the attention and provoking the curiosity of the reader." After the poets and novelists, the works of standard historians should be read with a view to surprising the secrets of their style — Herodotus, Thucydides, Xenophon, Polybius, and Plutarch; Cæsar, Sallust, Livy, and Tacitus; and, among the moderns, Macchiavelli, Guicciardini, Giannone, Hume, Robertson, Gibbon, and Voltaire. When the foundations of an elegant literary style are firmly established, the student may re-read the standard treatises with attention to the *matter* rather than the *form;* for, as even the judicious Daunou concedes, before writing history "it is evidently necessary to know it." Both Daunou's program and his list of names — unquestionably the most distinguished among historians throughout the centuries — testify to the strength of literary traditions among historical writers.

Yet a formal distinction at least has of course always been made between history and other branches of literature. This is emphasized by Polybius, writing in the second century before Christ. "Surely," he says, "an historian's object should be not to amaze his readers by a series of thrilling anecdotes, nor should he aim to produce speeches which *might* have been delivered, nor to study dramatic propriety in detail, like a writer of tragedy. On the contrary, his function is, above all, to record with fidelity what was actually said or done, no matter how commonplace it may be."

These warnings of Polybius were, however, commonly neglected by the ancient historian, whose object was to interest his readers in the great men and striking events of the past, or to prepare him for public life by describing and analyzing the policy of former statesmen and generals, or to teach him to bear with dignity the vicissitudes of fortune by recalling the calamities of others. It is clear that these ends of amusing, instructing, or edifying were to be attained mainly by literary skill rather than by painful historical research.

To Thucydides, Polybius, and Tacitus, history appeared to be purely human and secular. Its significance was confined to this world. To them any allusion to the influence of the gods or to providence would have seemed quite out of place. But with the establishment of the Christian church the past began to take on a religious and theological meaning.

II

To the early Christians Hebrew history, as narrated in the Old Testament, served as a very important substantiation and illustration of their contention that the Messiah had at last come. By means of allegorical interpretation the most casual episodes of

a remote past could be given a vivid and essential relation to the present.   The Christians were perhaps the
first to suspect a real grandeur in history, for to them
it became a divine epic, stretching back to the creation
of man and forward to the final separation of the good
and evil in a last magnificent and decisive crisis.

But this theological unity and meaning of history
was won at the tremendous sacrifice of all secular perspective and accuracy.   The Amorites were invested
with an importance denied the Carthaginians.   Enoch
and Lot loomed large in a past which scarcely knew of
a Pericles.   Allegory rendered all literary or historical
criticism irrelevant, if not an impious questioning of
God's own revealed truth.   Then Augustine came to
give an elaborate and plausible form to his theory of
two cities, — a City of God which had existed from the
first and which could be traced through the Old Testament into the New, and a City of Satan, founded by
the fallen angels, exemplified in King Belus and Queen
Semiramis, and trailing its obscene existence down
through the Roman Empire to his own day.   History
became sacred and profane.   The fantastically interpreted Jewish records, continued in the story of Christian martyrs and miracles, constituted history *par
excellence*.

All the achievements of Egypt, Greece, and Rome
tended to sink out of sight in the mind of Augustine's disciple, Orosius; only the woes of a devil-
worshiping heathendom lingered.   At Augustine's

suggestion he prepared his *Seven Books of History directed against the Pagans*. His aim was to refute those heathen detractors of Christianity who maintained that their age was accursed above all others, owing to the desertion of the ancient gods. He boldly maintained that, on the contrary, a veritable carnival of death had preceded the appearance of Christianity. To prove this he brought together, as he tells us, in the compass of a single volume, all the examples he could find in the annals of the past "of the most signal horrors of war, pestilence, and famine, of the fearful devastations of earthquakes and inundations, the destruction wrought by fiery eruptions, by lightning and hail, and the awful misery due to crime." His convenient and edifying treatise became the standard manual of universal history for a thousand years to follow. It was agreeable reading to medieval Christians, and it enjoyed the sanction of the chief among the church fathers. History thus became for Orosius, and for his innumerable readers in succeeding centuries, the story of God's punishment of sin and of the curse which man's original transgression had brought upon the whole earth.

But we need not expose ourselves to the hot and withering blasts of Orosius's rhetoric in order to realize the salient contrast between his conception of history's purpose and usefulness, and that of the classical Greek and Roman writers. In the old days the danger had been that Clio would fall into the way of aping her sisters, Poetry and the Drama, and of borrowing their finery. Now, she permitted herself to be led away blindfolded by Theology, which was for so long to be the potent rival of literature. The Greek historians and the greatest of the Romans, Tacitus, were forgotten in the Middle Ages; so the polemical pamphlet of Orosius served to distort Europe's vision of the past for a thousand years until Thucydides and Polybius came once more within its ken.

But even the revival of classical learning by no means put an end to the "providential" conception of the past. This finds beautiful expression in Bossuet's *Universal History*. He perceives behind all the great events which he recalls, the secret ordering of Providence : —

Dieu tient du plus haut des cieux les rênes de tous les royaumes ; il a tous les cœurs en sa main ; tantôt il retient les passions, tantôt il leur lâche la bride, et par là il remue tout le genre humain. Veut-il faire des conquérants ; il fait marcher l'épouvante devant eux, et il inspire à eux et à leurs soldats une hardiesse invincible. Veut-il faire des législateurs ; il leur envoie son esprit de sagesse et de prévoyance ; il leur fait prévenir les maux qui menacent les états, et poser les fondements de la tranquillité publique. Il connôit la sagesse humaine, toujours courte par quelque endroit ; il l'éclaire, il étend ses vues, et puis l'abandonne à ses ignorances ; il l'aveugle, il la précipite, il la confond par elle-même ; elle s'enveloppe, elle s'embarrasse dans ses propres subtilités, et ses précautions lui sont un piége. Dieu exerce par ce moyen ses redoutables jugements, selon les régles de sa justice toujours infaillible. [1]

[1] *Discours sur l'histoire universelle*, concluding chapter.

Unhappily the mysterious character of divine dispensations opened the door to conflicting views of their meaning. All history seemed to Bossuet to exhibit God's constant solicitude for the Catholic Church and his anger against all who swerved from the faith delivered to Peter and handed down by his successors. Luther, on the other hand, believed that History supported him in his attack upon what he called the "Teufels Nest zu Rom." And not long after his death a group of Protestants had compiled a vast history of the church — *The Magdeburg Centuries*, as it was called — in which they sought to prove the diabolical origin of the papacy and of the Roman Catholic Church. Cardinal Baronius replied in twelve folio volumes, written, as he trusted, under the direct auspices of the Virgin Mary, in which he set forth "the calamities divinely sent for the punishment of those who have dared to oppose in their arrogance, or conspire against, the true church of God." For three centuries each party continued to suborn history in its own interest, and one must still, to-day, allow for religious bias in important fields of historical research. Yet in spite of all their bitterness and blindness, religious controversies have stimulated much scholarly investigation in modern times, and we should be much poorer if certain works of a distinctly partisan character had never been written, — such, for example, as Raynaldus' continuation of Baronius and, in our own days, Janssen's *History of the German People*.

D

To the authors of the *Magdeburg Centuries* and to Cardinal Baronius — to Protestant and Catholic historians alike — the great, obvious, determining historical forces were God and the devil. Our conception of God, as well as our ideas of history, have, however, been changing since the sixteenth century, and it is rare now to find a historian who possesses the old confidence in his ability to penetrate God's counsels and trace his dispensations in detail. As for the devil, few events can longer be ascribed to him with perfect assurance.

III

The reversion to the worldly standards of historical composition, represented by Macchiavelli and Guicciardini in the early sixteenth century, became pronounced in the eighteenth. Gibbon, Voltaire, Hume, Robertson, and others successfully resecularized history and strove to give their narrative of political events the ancient elegance of form.

Lord Bolingbroke, in his *Letters on the Study of History*, written about 1737, says: "An application to any study that tends neither to make us better men and better citizens is at best but a specious and ingenious sort of idleness; . . . and the knowledge we acquire by it is a creditable kind of ignorance, nothing more. This creditable kind of ignorance is, in my opinion, the whole benefit which the generality of men, even the most learned, reap from the study of history : and yet the study of history seems to me of all others the most proper to train us up to private and public virtue." History, he quite properly says, is read by most people as a form of amusement, as they might play at cards. Some devote themselves to history in order to adorn their conversation with historical allusions, — and the argument is still current that one should know enough of the past to understand literary references to noteworthy events and persons. The less imaginative scholar, Bolingbroke complains, satisfies himself with making fair copies of foul manuscripts and explaining hard words for the benefit of others, or with constructing more or less fantastic chronologies based upon very insecure data. Over against these Bolingbroke places those who have perceived that history is after all only "philosophy teaching by example." For "the examples which we find in history, improved by the lively descriptions and the just explanations or censures of historians," will, he believes, have a much better and more permanent effect than declamation, or the "dry ethics of mere philosophy." Moreover, to summarize his argument, we can by the study of history enjoy in a short time a wide range of experience at the expense of other men and without risk to ourselves. History enables us "to live with the men who lived before us, and we inhabit countries that we never saw. Place is enlarged, and time prolonged in this manner : so that the man who applies himself early to the study of history may acquire in a few years, and before he sets foot in the world, not only a more extended knowledge of mankind, but the experience of more centuries than any of the patriarchs saw." Our own personal experience is doubly defective; we are born too late to see the beginning, and we die too soon to see the end of many things. History supplies in a large measure these defects.

There is, of course, little originality in Bolingbroke's plea for history's usefulness in making wiser and better men and citizens. Polybius had seen in history a guide for statesmen and military commanders; and the hope that the striking moral victories and defeats of the past would serve to arouse virtue and discourage vice has been urged by innumerable chroniclers as the main justification of their enterprises. To-day, however, one rarely finds a historical student who would venture to recommend statesmen, warriors, and moralists to place any confidence whatsoever in historical analogies and warnings, for the supposed analogies usually prove illusive on inspection, and the warnings, impertinent. Whether or no Napoleon was ever able to make any practical use in his own campaigns of the accounts he had read of those of Alexander and Cæsar, it is quite certain that Admiral Togo would have derived no useful hints from Nelson's tactics at Alexandria or Trafalgar. Our situation is so novel that it would seem as if political and military precedents of even a century ago could have no possible value. As

for our present "anxious morality," as Maeterlinck
calls it, it seems equally clear that the sinful extravagances of Sardanapalus and Nero, and the conspicuous
public virtue of Aristides and the Horatii, are alike
impotent to promote it.

In the eighteenth century a considerable number of
"philosophies of history" appeared and enjoyed great
popularity. They were the outcome of a desire to
seize and explain the general trend of man's past. Of
course this had been also the purpose of Augustine
and Bossuet, but Voltaire devoted his *Philosophie de
l'histoire* (1765) mainly to discrediting religion as
commonly accepted; and instead of offering any particular theory of the past he satisfied himself with picking out what he calls "les vérités utiles." He addresses
Madame du Châtelet in the opening of his *Essai sur
les Mœurs et l'esprit des nations* as follows: —

Vous ne cherchez dans cette immensité que ce qui mérite
d'être connu de vous; l'esprit, les mœurs, les usages des
nations principales, appuyés des faits qu'il n'est pas permis
d'ignorer. Le but de ce travail n'est pas de savoir en quelle
année un prince indigne d'être connu succéda à un prince
barbare chez une nation grossière. Si l'on pouvait avoir le
malheur de mettre dans sa tête la suite chronologique de toutes
les dynasties, on ne saurait que des mots. Autant il faut connaître les grandes actions des souverains qui ont rendu leurs
peuples meilleurs et plus heureux, autant on peut ignorer le
vulgaire des rois, qui ne pourrait que charger la mémoire. . . .
Dans tous ces recueils immenses qu'on ne peut embrasser, il
faut se borner et choisir. C'est un vaste magazin où vous
prendrez ce qui est à votre usage.

Voltaire's reactions on the past were naturally just what might have been expected from his attitude toward his own times. He drew from "le vaste magazin" those things that he needed for his great campaign, and in this he did well, however uncritical his criticism may seem at times to a modern historical student.

Herder in his little work, *Auch eine Philosophie der Geschichte zur Bildung der Menschheit. Beitrag zur vielen Beitragen des Jahrhunderts* (1774), condemns the general light-heartedness and superficiality of Voltaire and other contemporary writers who were, he thought, vainly attempting to squeeze the story of the universe and man into their puny philosophic categories. Ten years later he wrote his larger work, *Ideen zur Geschichte der Menschheit*, in which he strove to give some ideal unity and order to the vast historic process, beginning with a consideration of the place of the earth among the other heavenly bodies, and of man's relations to the vegetable and animal kingdoms. "If," he says, "there be a god in nature, there is in history too; for man is himself a part of creation, and in his wildest extravagances and passions must obey laws not less excellent and beautiful than those by which all the celestial bodies move. Now, as I am persuaded that man is capable of knowing, and destined to attain the knowledge of, everything that he ought to know, I step freely and confidently from the tumultuous scenes through which we have been wandering, to inspect the beautiful and sublime laws of nature by which they have been governed." Humanity is the end of human nature, he held, and the human race is destined to proceed through various degrees of civilization in various mutations; but the permanency of its welfare is founded solely and essentially on reason and justice. It is, moreover, a natural law that "if a being or system of beings be forced out of the permanent position of its truth, goodness, and beauty, it will again approach it by its internal powers, either in vibrations or in an asymptote, since out of this state it finds no stability." Herder formulates from time to time a considerable number of other "laws" which he believes emerge from the confusion of the past. Whatever we may think of these "laws," he constantly astonishes the modern reader not only by his penetrating criticism of the prevailing philosophy of his time, but by flashes of deep historical insight. He is clearly enough the forerunner of the "Romantic" tendency that culminated in Hegel's celebrated *Philosophy of History*.

IV

Since the middle of the eighteenth century, new interests other than the more primitive literary, political, military, moral, and theological, have been developing. These have exercised a remarkable influence upon historical research, radically altering its spirit and aims and broadening its scope. To take a single example, Montesquieu's *Spirit of Laws* — first published in 1748 — reviews the past with the purpose of establishing a purely scientific proposition, namely, the relativity of all human institutions, social, political, educational, economic, legal, and military. The discussions attending the drafting of the first French Constitution (1789–1791) served to provoke a study of constitutional history which has never since flagged.

Early in the nineteenth century the cosmopolitan sentiments so conspicuous at the opening of the French Revolution began to give way to the spirit of nationality which was awaking in the various European states, especially in Germany. This almost immediately showed itself in a new and highly characteristic interpretation of the philosophy of history. Although the writer makes no pretensions to understanding Hegel, it may be worth while to repeat a few things he said in his lectures on the philosophy of history, first delivered in Berlin in the winter of 1822–1823, for many people have thought they did understand him and were deeply affected by his teachings. As he looked back over the restless mutations of individuals and peoples, existing for a time and then vanishing, he was confident that he could trace the World-Spirit striving for consciousness and then for freedom, its essential nature. This spirit assumes successive forms which it successively transcends. These forms are exhibited in the peculiar natural genius of historic peoples. The spirit of a particular people, having strictly defined characteristics, "erects itself," Hegel explains, "into an objective world that exists and persists in a particular form of religious worship, customs, constitution and political laws,—in short, in the whole complex of its institutions, and in the events and transactions that make up its history." The Persians, Hegel held, were the first world-historical people, for was it not in Persia that the World-Spirit first began to attain an "unlimited immanence of subjectivity"? The Greek character was "individuality conditioned by beauty." "Subjective inwardness" was the general principle of the Roman world. Ingenious as this theory may be, it would hardly have formed the basis of a new gospel of national freedom and deeply affected historical interpretation, had it not been for Hegel's extraordinary discovery that it was his own dear German nation in which it had pleased the "Weltgeist" to assume its highest form. "The German Spirit is the Spirit of the new world," Hegel proclaims; "its aim is the realization of absolute truth, as the unlimited self-determination of Freedom. . . . The destiny of the German peoples is to be the bearers of the Christian principle."

The supreme rôle assigned by Hegel to his own countrymen filled them with justifiable pride. And was not this assumption amply borne out by the glories of "Deutschthum" in the Middle Ages, which

the Romanticists were singing : and, much more recently, by the successful expulsion of the French
tyrant ?   That all this should combine to give a distinct national and patriotic trend to historic research
and writing was inevitable.   The great collection of
the sources for the German Middle Ages, — the "Mon-
umenta Germaniæ Historica" — which was to become
a model for other nations, began to be issued in 1826,
and for the first time the Germans became leaders in
the historical field as in so many others.   Ranke,
Dahn, Giesebrecht, Waitz, Droysen, and dozens of
others who began to devote themselves to German
history, were all filled with a warm patriotism and enthusiasm very different from the cosmopolitan spirit
of the preceding century.   Throughout Europe, history tended to become distinctly national, and an extraordinary impetus was given to the publication of
vast collections of material.

It was natural that this national spirit and the political and constitutional questions of the nineteenth
century should serve to perpetuate the older interest
in political history.   This is the most ancient, most
obvious, and easiest kind of history, for the policy of
kings, the laws they issued and the wars they fought,
have always been the matters which were likeliest to
be recorded.   Then the State is the most imposing
and important of man's social creations, and historians have commonly felt that what was best worth
knowing in the past could be directly or indirectly

associated with its history. Ranke, Droysen, Maurenbrecher, Freeman, and many others deemed political history to be history in its most unmistakable form.

V

We have now reviewed the chief motives which appear to have influenced the greater number of historical writers from Thucydides to Macaulay and Ranke. They all agreed in examining more or less conscientiously and critically the records of past events and conditions with a view to amusing, edifying, or comforting the reader. But none of the main interests of which I have so far spoken can be regarded as scientific. To scan the past with the hope of discovering recipes for the making of statesmen and warriors, of discrediting the pagan gods, of showing that Catholic or Protestant is right, of exhibiting the stages of self-realization of the *Weltgeist*, or demonstrating that Liberty emerged from the forests of Germany never to return thither, — none of these motives are scientific, although they may go hand in hand with much sound scholarship. But by the middle of the nineteenth century the Muse of History — *semper mutabile* — began to fall under the potent spell of natural science. She was no longer satisfied to celebrate the deeds of heroes and nations with the lyre and shrill flute on the breeze-swept slopes of Helicon; she no longer durst attempt to vindicate the ways of God to man. She came to recognize that she was ill-prepared for her undertakings, and began to spend her mornings in the library, collating manuscripts and making out lists of variant readings. She aspired to do even more, and began to talk of raising her chaotic mass of information to the rank of a science.

The results of history's new ambition to become scientific are of the greatest importance. In the first place the sources of information in regard to the past began to be viewed with critical suspicion. So long as historians continued to present to the reader such conspicuous events as they thought might enlist his interest, and commented on these with a view of fortifying his virtue or patriotism or staying his faith in God, it made little difference whether they took pains to verify the facts or not. Indeed, the exact truth, when we are lucky enough to get a glimpse of it, is rarely so picturesque or so edifying as "what might have been." But to-day a large part of the historian's attention is directed to the character, reliability, or defects of his sources. The data upon which history rests have been subjected to the most searching scrutiny. Much that was formerly relied upon has either been partially rejected or thrown out altogether; but much has also been added by scrupulous search and systematic cataloguing.

Moreover, the historian now realizes clearly that all his sources of information are inferior, in their very nature, to data available in the various fields of natural science. He can almost never have any direct experience of the phenomena which he describes. He only knows the facts of the past by the imperfect traces they have left, whether in books, documents, inscriptions, or in the remains of buildings and other archæological survivals. The traces he finds in books — upon which he has been wont to rely chiefly — are usually only the reports of some one who commonly did not himself have any direct experience of the facts and who did not even take the trouble to tell us where he got his alleged information. This is true of almost all the ancient and medieval historians and annalists. So it comes about that "the immense majority of the sources of information which furnish the historian with startling points for his reasoning are nothing else than traces of psychological operations" rather than direct traces of facts. As a French scholar has remarked, the historian is in the position of a chemist who should be forced to rely for his knowledge of a series of experiments upon what his laboratory boy tells him.

To take a single example from among thousands which might be cited: Gibbon tells us that after the death of Alaric in 410 "the ferocious character of the Barbarians was displayed in the funeral of the hero, whose valor and fortune they celebrated with mournful applause. By the labor of a captive multitude they forcibly diverted the course of the Busen-

tinus, a small river that washes the walls of Consentia.
The royal sepulcher, adorned with the splendid spoils
and trophies of Rome, was constructed in the vacant
bed; the waters were then restored to their natural
channel, and the secret spot where the remains of
Alaric had been deposited, was forever concealed by
the inhuman massacre of the prisoners who had been
employed to execute the work." The basis of this
account is the illiterate *History of the Goths* written
by an ignorant person, Jordanes, about a hundred
and forty years after the occurrence of the supposed
events. We know that Jordanes copied freely from
a work of his better-instructed contemporary, Cassiodorus, which has been lost. This is absolutely
all we know about the sources of our information.

Shall we believe this story, which has found its way
into so many of our textbooks? Gibbon did not
witness the burial of Alaric, nor did Jordanes, upon
whose tale Gibbon greatly improves, nor did Cassiodorus, who was not born until some eighty years after
the death of the Gothic king. We can control the
"psychological operation" represented in Gibbon's
text, for he says he got the tale from Jordanes, but,
aside from our suspicion that Jordanes took the story
from the lost book by Cassiodorus, we have no means of
controlling the various psychological operations which
separate the tale as we have it from the real circumstances. We have other reasons than Jordanes'
authority for supposing that Alaric is dead; as for the

circumstances of his burial we can only say they may have been as described but we have only the slightest reason for supposing that they were.

VI

A second general result of the scientific spirit may be detected in Ranke's proud boast that he proposed to tell the truth, — *wie es eigentlich gewesen.* This modest ambition appears to have needed some apology in the middle of the nineteenth century. Previous historians, as has been explained, often had other dominating motives, and history was expected to support, or at least not run counter to, prevailing patriotic and religious prejudices. A conscious resolve, therefore, to state the facts as he found them has certainly placed the historian on a far higher plane than he formerly occupied, and has been revolutionary in its effects. For example, a wide range of religious phenomena has been subjected to really scientific examination during the past fifty years, with the most startling results.

But to resolve to test one's sources carefully and to state only what seems to be supported by adequate evidence are, after all, only the bare preliminaries of scientific historiography. The quantity of facts about the past of man which are susceptible of satisfactory verification not only far exceeds the compass of any possible single presentation, but they are so heterogeneous in their character as to invite a great variety of interpretations. In what ways, we may accordingly ask next, has the potent influence of natural science affected historical writers in the choice of facts to put before the reader and in the explanations and interpretations which they tender him?

First, what are the most striking traits of modern scientific method? It may be confidently replied that an appreciation of the overwhelming significance of the small, the common, and the obscure, and an unhesitating rejection of all theological, supernatural, and anthropocentric explanations, establish the brotherhood of all scientific workers, whatever their fields of research. Then there is the search for natural laws and their multiform applications which has proved fruitful beyond the wildest expectations of the most sanguine. Minute and patient investigation, the discovery of natural explanations and of natural laws, constitute, then, the most salient features of modern scientific research.

History has so long been concealed behind a mask which served either to enhance the charm of her homely features beyond all recognition, or to render her familiar and commonplace form monstrous and repulsive, that it is little wonder that historians only slowly adjust themselves to the scientific point of view. The older historians had little inclination to describe familiar conditions and the common routine of daily life. It was the startling and exceptional that caught their attention and which they found recorded in the sources on which they depended. They were like a geologist who should deal only with earthquakes and volcanoes, or, better still, a zoölogist who should have no use for anything smaller than an elephant or less romantic in its habits than a phœnix or a basilisk. The modernizing of history has taken place much more slowly and much more recently than the disentangling of chemistry from alchemy and of astronomy from the dreams of the astrologer. Perhaps Buckle was right when he declared that the historians have been, on the whole, inferior in point of intellect to thinkers in other fields, but it should not be forgotten that their task is beset with peculiar and well-nigh insurmountable difficulties, when compared with the problems of chemistry or geology. It is no wonder that the historian's gradual escape from ancient misapprehensions is largely attributable not to his own efforts, but to the general influence of natural science and to the specific influence of the various social sciences which have made their appearance from time to time.[1]

The first social science greatly to affect the selection of historical facts and their interpretation was, not unnaturally, Political Economy, which developed during the eighteenth century. It was not a pro-

[1] The relation of history to these newer social sciences is the subject of the essay which follows this.

E

fessional student of history, but an economist, who first suggested a new and wonderful series of questions which the historian might properly ask about the past, and, moreover, furnished him with a scientific explanation of many matters hitherto ill-understood.

As early as 1845, Karl Marx denounced those who discover the birthplace of history in the shifting clouds of heaven instead of in the hard, daily work on earth. He maintained that the only sound and ever valid explanation of the past must be economic. The history of society depends, he held, upon the methods by which its members produce their means of support and exchange the products of industry among themselves. The methods of production and transportation determine the methods of exchange, the distribution of products, the division of society into classes, the relations of the several classes, the existence of the State, the character of its laws, and all that it means for mankind.

We are not concerned here with the complicated genesis of this idea, nor with the precise degree of originality to be attributed to Marx's presentation of it. Nor is there time to explain the manner in which Marx's theory was misused by himself and his followers. Few, if any, historians would agree that everything can be explained economically, as many of the socialists and some economists of good standing would have us believe. But in the sobered and chastened form in which most economists now accept the doctrine, it serves to explain far more of the phenomena of the past than any other single explanation ever offered. In any case, it is the economist who has opened up the most fruitful new fields of research by emphasizing the importance of those enduring but often inconspicuous factors which almost entirely escaped historians before the middle of the nineteenth century. The essential interest and importance of the normal and homely elements in human life have become apparent. The scientific historian no longer dwells by preference on the heroic, spectacular, and romantic episodes, but strives to reconstruct past conditions. This last point is so significant that we must stop over it a moment.

History is not infrequently still defined as a record of past events, and the public still expect from the historian a story of the past. But the conscientious historian has come to realize that he cannot aspire to be a good story-teller for the simple reason that, if he tells no more than he has good reason for believing to be true, his tale is usually very fragmentary and vague. Fiction and drama are perfectly free to conceive and adjust detail so as to meet the demands of art, but the historian should always be conscious of the rigid limitations placed upon him. If he confines himself to an honest and critical statement of a series of events as described in his sources, it is usually too deficient in vivid authentic detail to make a satisfactory story.

The historian is coming to see that his task is essentially different from that of the man of letters, and that his place is rather among the scientists. He is at liberty to use only his scientific imagination, which is quite different from a literary imagination. It is his business to make those contributions to our general understanding of mankind in the past which his training in the investigation of the records of past human events especially fit him to make. He esteems the events he finds recorded, not for their dramatic interest, but for the light that they cast on the normal and generally prevalent conditions which gave rise to them. It makes no difference how dry a chronicle may be if the occurrences that it reports can be brought into some assignable relation with the more or less permanent habits and environment of a particular people or person. If it be the chief function of history to show how things come about, — and something has already been said of this matter,[1] — then events become for the historian, first and foremost, evidence of general conditions and of changes affecting considerable numbers of people. In this respect history is only following the example set by the older natural sciences: Zoölogy, for instance, dwells on general principles, not on exceptional and startling creatures or on the lessons which their habits suggest for man ; Mathematics no longer lingers over the mystic qualities of numbers, nor

[1] See above, pp. 18 *sqq.*

does the astronomer seek to read our individual fate in the positions of the planets. But scientific truth has shown itself able to compete with fiction, and there is endless fascination for the modern mind in the contemplation of what former ages would have regarded as the most vulgar and tiresome commonplace.

It was inevitable that attempts would be made to reduce history to a science by seeking for its laws and by reconstructing it upon the lines suggested by the natural sciences. The most celebrated instance of this is Buckle's uncompleted *History of Civilization*, the first volume of which appeared in 1857. It seemed to him that while the historical material which had been collected, when looked at in the aggregate, had "a rich and imposing appearance," the real problem of the historian had hardly been suspected, let alone solved. "For all the higher purposes of human thought," he declares, "history is still miserably deficient, and presents that confused and anarchical appearance natural to a subject of which the laws are unknown and even the foundations unsettled." He accordingly hoped, he tells us, to "accomplish for the history of man something equivalent, or at all events analogous, to what has been effected by other inquirers for the different branches of natural science. In regard to nature, events apparently the most irregular and capricious have been explained, and have been shown to be in accordance with certain fixed and universal laws. This has been done because men of ability, and, above all, men of patient, untiring thought, have studied natural events with the view of discovering their regularity; and if human events were subjected to a similar treatment, we have every right to expect similar results." Buckle proposed to discover the laws, physical and mental, which govern the workings of mankind, and then trace their operations in the general development of civilization. Unlike Marx, Buckle believed that physical laws tended to become well-nigh inoperative in so highly developed a civilization as that of Europe, and that, consequently, moral and intellectual laws should constitute the main object of the historian's search.

Fifty years have elapsed since Buckle's book appeared, and I know of no historian who would venture to maintain that we had made any considerable advance toward the goal he set for himself. A systematic prosecution of the various branches of social science, especially political economy, sociology, anthropology, and psychology, is succeeding in explaining many things; but history must always remain, from the standpoint of the astronomer, physicist, or chemist, a highly inexact and fragmentary body of knowledge. This is due mainly to the fact that it concerns itself with man, his devious ways and wandering desires, which it seems hopeless at present to bring within the compass of clearly defined laws of any kind. Then our historical knowledge, as we have seen, must forever rest upon scattered and highly precarious data, the truth of which we have often no means of testing. History can no doubt be pursued in a strictly scientific spirit, but the data we possess in regard to the past of mankind are not of a nature to lend themselves to organization into an exact science, although, as we shall see, they may yield truths of vital importance.

The modern historical student is well aware of the treacherous nature of his materials and their woeful inadequacy, but even conscientious scholars have been accustomed, in writing for the public, to disguise their doubts and uncertainties. The exigencies of effective literary presentation have forced them to conceal their pitiful ignorance and yield to the temptation to ignore yawning chasms of nescience at whose brink heavy-footed History is forced to halt, although Literature is able to transcend them at a leap. It is largely an exaggerated and altogether false notion of the extent of our knowledge that has encouraged the reckless ventures of those who, like Buckle and Draper, have dreamed of reducing history to an exact science.

Fifty years ago it was generally believed that we knew something about man from the very beginning. Of his abrupt appearance on the freshly created earth and his early conduct, there appeared to be a brief but exceptionally authoritative account. To-day we are beginning to recognize the immense antiquity of man. There are paleolithic implements which there is some reason for supposing may have been made a hundred or two hundred thousand years ago ; the eolithic remains recently discovered may perhaps antedate the paleolithic by an equally long period. These are mere guesses and impressions, of course, — this assignment of millenniums, which appear to have been preceded by some hundreds of thousands of years during which an animal was developing with "a relatively enormous brain case, a skillful hand, and an inveterate tendency to throw stones, flourish sticks," and in general, as Ray Lankester expresses it, "to defeat aggression and satisfy his natural appetites by the use of his wits rather than by strength alone." There may still be historians who would argue that all this has nothing to do with history, — that it is "prehistoric." But "prehistoric" is a word that must go the way of "preadamite," which we used to hear. They both indicate a suspicion that we are in some way gaining illicit information about what happened before the footlights were turned on and the curtain rose on the great human drama. Of the so-called "prehistoric" period we, of course, know as yet very little indeed, but the bare fact that there was such a period constitutes in itself the most momentous of historical discoveries. The earliest traces of an elaborate and advanced stage of human civilization — found in the Nile valley — can hardly be placed earlier than six thousand years ago. It is quite gratuitous, however, to assume that this was the first time that man had risen to such a stage of culture.

Let us suppose that there has been something worth saying about the deeds and progress of mankind during the past three hundred thousand years at least; let us suppose that we were fortunate enough to have the merest outline of such changes as have overtaken our race during that period, and that a single page were devoted to each thousand years. Of the three hundred pages of our little manual the closing six or seven only would be allotted to the whole period for which records, in the ordinary sense of the word, exist, even in the scantiest and most fragmentary form. Or, to take another illustration, let us imagine history under the semblance of a vast lake into whose rather turbid depths we eagerly peer. We have reason to think it at least twenty-five feet deep, perhaps fifty or a hundred. We detect the very scantiest indications of life, *rara et disjecta*, four or five feet beneath the surface; six or seven inches down, these are abundant, but at that depth we can detect, so to speak, no movements of animate things, which are scarcely perceptible below three or four inches. If we are frank with ourselves, we shall have to admit that we can have no clear and adequate notion of anything happening more than an inch — indeed, scarce more than half an inch — below the surface.

From this point of view the historian's gaze, instead of sweeping back into remote ages when the earth was young, seems to be confined to his own epoch; Rameses II, Tiglath-Pileser, and Solomon appear

practically coeval with Cæsar, Constantine, Charlemagne, St. Louis, Charles V, and Victoria; Bacon,
Newton, and Darwin are but the younger contemporaries of Thales, Plato, and Aristotle. Let those pause
who would attempt to determine the laws of human
progress or decay. It is like trying to determine, by
observing the conduct of a man of forty for a week,
whether he be developing or not. Anything approaching an adequate record of events does not reach back
for more than three thousand years, and even this
remains distressingly imperfect and unreliable for more
than two millenniums. We have a few, often highly
fragmentary, literary histories covering Greek and
Roman times, also a good many inscriptions and some
important archæological remains; but these leave us
in the dark upon many vital matters. The sources
for the Roman Empire are so very bad that Mommsen
refused to attempt to write its history. Only in the
twelfth and thirteenth centuries do the medieval
annals and chronicles begin to be supplemented by
miscellaneous documents which bring us more directly
into contact with the life of the time.

Yet the reader of history must often get the impression that the sources of our knowledge are, so to speak,
of a uniform volume and depth, at least for the last
two or three thousand years. When he beholds a
voluminous account of the early Church, or of the
Roman Empire, or observes Dahn's or Hodgkin's
many stately volumes on the Barbarian invasions,

he is to be pardoned for assuming that the writers
have spent years in painfully condensing and giving
literary form to the abundant material which they
have turned up in the course of their prolonged researches. Too few suspect that it has been the business of the historian in the past not to condense but,
on the contrary, skillfully to inflate his thin film of
knowledge until the bubble should reach such proportions that its bright hues would attract the attention
and elicit the admiration of even the most careless
observer. One volume of Hodgkin's rather old-fash-
ioned *Italy and her Invaders*, had the scanty material
been judiciously compressed, might have held all that
we can be said to even half know about the matters to
which the author has seen fit to devote eight volumes.

But one should not jump to the conclusion that the
historical writer is a sinner above all men. In the
first place, it should never be forgotten that he is by
long tradition a man of letters, and that that is not,
after all, such a bad thing to be. In the second place,
he experiences the same strong temptation that every
one else does to accept at their face value the plausible statements which he finds, unless they conflict
with other accounts of the same events, or appear to
be inherently improbable. Lastly, he is, like his fellow
primates, the victim of what Nietzsche has called
"dream logic." I am sure that we do not reckon constantly enough with this inveterate tendency of even
a highly cultivated mind instinctively to elaborate

and amplify mere hints and suggestions into complete and vivid pictures.

To take an illustration of Nietzsche's, the vague feeling, as we lie in bed, that the soles of our feet are free from the usual pressure to which we are accustomed in our waking hours demands an explanation. Our dream explanation is that we are flying. Not satisfied to leave its work half done, dream logic fabricates a room or landscape in which we make our aërial experiments. Moreover, just as we are going to sleep or awaking we can often actually observe how a flash of light, such as sometimes appears on the retina of our closed eyes, will be involuntarily interpreted as a vision of some human figure or other object, clear as a stereopticon slide. Now any one can demonstrate to himself that neither dream logic nor the "mind's-eye faculty," as it has been called, deserts us when we are awake. Indeed they may well be, as Nietzsche suspects, a portion of the inheritance bequeathed to us, along with some other inconveniences, by our brutish forebears. At any rate they are forms of aberration against which the historian, with his literary traditions, needs specially to be on his guard. There are rumors that even the student of natural science sometimes keeps his "mind's eye" too wide open, but he is by no means so likely as the historian to be misled by dream logic. This is not to be ascribed necessarily to the superior self-restraint of the scientist, but rather to the greater simplicity of his task and the palpableness of much of his knowledge.

It is essential, as has been pointed out, for every one dealing with the past of mankind to understand that history can never become a science in the sense that physics, chemistry, physiology, or even anthropology, is a science. The complexity of the phenomena is appalling, and we have no way of observing them directly, to say nothing of artificially analyzing and experimenting with our facts. We know absolutely nothing of the occurrences in the history of mankind during a great part of his existence on the earth, and only since the invention of printing do our sources become in any sense abundant. Writers trained in the natural sciences, who have attempted to show historians how to use their material, have commonly quite misunderstood the situation and the conditions under which the historian has necessarily to work.[1]

[1] For example, Dr. Draper, in his well-known *Intellectual Development of Europe*, undertook to prove two great truths which he believed had escaped the historians : that " social advancement is as completely under the control of natural law as is bodily growth," and that "the life of an individual is a miniature of the life of a nation." Nowhere does he suggest that he exercised the least care in collecting the evidence for these hazardous propositions; nowhere in his volumes does he allude to any sources of information in regard to a past which he claims to interpret in its scientific relations. Not long ago a Boston physician published a work on heredity in which he denounces the utter superficiality of historians and then proceeds to build up a theory of royal heredity based on the data found in that ancient household convenience, Thomas's *Biographical Dictionary*.

VII

But history, in order to become scientific, had first to become historical. Singularly enough, what we now regard as the strictly historical interest was almost missed by historians before the nineteenth century. They narrated such past events as they believed would interest the reader; they commented on these with a view of instructing him. They took some pains to find out how things really were — *wie es eigentlich gewesen.* To this extent they were scientific, although their motives were mainly literary, moral, or religious. They did not, however, in general try to determine how things had come about — *wie es eigentlich geworden.* History has remained for two or three thousand years mainly a record of past events, and this definition satisfies the thoughtless still. But it is one thing to describe what once was; it is still another to attempt to determine how it came about.

It is impossible here to trace the causes and gradual development of this genetic interest. The main reason for its present strength lies probably in our modern lively consciousness of the reality and inevitability of change, examples of which are continually forcing themselves upon our attention. The Greek historians had little or no background for their narratives. It is amazing to note the contemptuous manner in which Thucydides rejects all accounts of even the immediately preceding generations, as mere uncertain traditions. Polybius set himself the task of tracing the gradual extension of the Roman dominion, but there is no indication that he had any clear idea of the continuity of history. In the Middle Ages there was undoubtedly a notion that the earth was the scene of a divine drama which was to have its dénouement in the definitive separation of the wheat from the tares; but this supernatural unity of history was not scientific but theological. In earthly matters the medieval man could hardly have understood the meaning of the word "anachronism"; the painters of the Renaissance did not hesitate to place a crucifix over the manger of the divine infant, and there appears to have been nothing incongruous in this to their contemporaries.

Not until the eighteenth century did the possibility of indefinite human progress become the exhilarating doctrine of reformers, a class which had previously attacked existing abuses in the name of the "good old times." No discovery could be more momentous and fundamental than that reform should seek its sanction in the future, not in the past; in advance, not in reaction.[1] It became clearer and clearer that the world *did* change, and by the middle of the nineteenth century the continuity of history began to be accepted by the more thoughtful students of the past, and began to affect, as never before, their motives and methods of research.

[1] See the final essay in this volume, on "The Spirit of Conservatism in the Light of History."

The doctrine of the continuity of history is based upon the observed fact that every human institution, every generally accepted idea, every important invention, is but the summation of long lines of progress, reaching back as far as we have the patience or means to follow them. The jury, the drama, the Gatling gun, the papacy, the letter *S*, the doctrine of *stare decisis*, each owes its present form to antecedents which can be scientifically traced. But no human interest is isolated from innumerable concurrent interests and conditioning circumstances. This brings us to the broader conception of the continuity of change which is attributable to the complexity of men's affairs. A somewhat abrupt change may take place in some single institution or habit, but a sudden general change is almost inconceivable. An individual may, through some modification of his environment, through bereavement or malignant disease, be quickly and fundamentally metamorphosed, but even such cases are rare. If all the habits and interests of the individual are considered, it will be found that only in the most exceptional cases are any great number of these altered in the twinkling of an eye. And society for obvious reasons is infinitely more conservative than the individual. Now — and this cannot be too strongly emphasized — the continuity of history is a scientific truth, the attempt to trace the slow process of change is a scientific problem, and one of the most fascinating in its nature. It is the discovery and application of this law which has served to differentiate history from literature and morals, and which has raised it, in one sense, to the dignity of a science.

VIII

The rapidly developing specialization in history, which is the result of more exacting scientific standards, forces upon the historical student a new and fundamental question. If all departments of knowledge have now become historical, what need is there of history in general? If politics, war, art, law, religion, science, literature, be dealt with genetically, will not history tend inevitably to disintegrate into its organic elements? Professor Seeley of the University of Cambridge believed that it would. Twenty years ago he declared that history was after all but the name of "a residuum which has been left when one group of facts after another has been taken possession of by some science; that residuum which now exists must go the way of the rest, and that time is not very distant when a science will take possession of the facts which are still the undisputed property of the historian."

Now the last question that I have to discuss is whether history, after gaining the whole world, is destined to lose her own soul. Let us assume that historical specialization has done its perfect work,

that every distinct phase of man's past, every institution, sentiment, conception, discovery, achievement, or defeat which is recorded has found its place
in the historical treatment of the particular branch of
research to which it has been assigned according to the
prevailing classification of the sciences. This process
of specialization would serve to rectify history in a
thousand ways, and to broaden and deepen its operations, but, instead of destroying it, it would rather
tend, on the contrary, to demonstrate with perfect
clearness its absolute indispensability. Human affairs
and human changes do not lend themselves to an
exhaustive treatment through a series of monographs
upon the ecclesiastical or military organization of
particular societies, their legal procedure, agrarian
system, their art, domestic habits, or views on higher
education. Many vital matters would prove highly
recalcitrant when one attempted to force them into
a neat, scientific cubby-hole. Physical, moral, and
intellectual phenomena are mysteriously interacting
in that process of life and change which it falls to
the historian to study and describe.

Man is far more than the sum of his scientifically
classifiable operations. Water is composed of hydro-
gen and oxygen, but it is not like either of them.
Nothing could be more artificial than the scientific
separation of man's religious, æsthetic, economic,
political, intellectual, and bellicose properties. These
may be studied, each by itself, with advantage, but

specialization would lead to the most absurd results if there were not some one to study the process as a whole; and that some one is the historian. Imagine the devotees of the various social sciences each engaged in describing his particular interest in the Crusades, or the Protestant Revolt, or the French Revolution. When they had finished, would not the historian have to retell the story, utilizing all that they had accomplished, including what they had all omitted, and rectifying the errors into which each of the specialists had fallen on account of his ignorance of the general situation?

It would seem at first sight as if those most familiar with each special subject of research — such as constitutional law, botany, theology, philology, painting, chemistry, economics, medicine — would be the only properly qualified persons to trace its history; but the scientific specialist is likely to suffer from two disadvantages. In the first place, his very familiarity with the principles of his particular branch of knowledge makes it difficult for him to conceive remote and unfamiliar conditions which historically lie back of the conceptions which he entertains. In the second place, the discovery, use, and interpretation of historical material seem to require a somewhat prolonged and special training, which only the professional historical student is likely to possess. He is constantly shocked by a certain awkwardness which those inexperienced in historical research are almost sure to betray. They make mistakes which he would not make, in spite of their greater knowledge of the subject with which they are dealing. This doubtless accounts for the fact that we have as yet no tolerably satisfactory history of natural science, or even of its special branches. There are, moreover, certain important phases of human thought and endeavor where the trained historian will have no particular difficulty in mastering the technical detail sufficiently to deal satisfactorily with them. Indeed, even the most subtle of the modern sciences, not excluding mathematics, were sufficiently simple two hundred years ago to enable a well-equipped historical student, with some taste for a particular human interest, to trace its development down until very recent times. So it may fall out, as time goes on, that historical students will tend to specialize more and more, and will supply the deficiency which students of contemporary branches of science are not ordinarily in a position to satisfy, — but more will be said on this subject, especially in regard to intellectual history, in a later essay.

I have frankly revealed the historian's ignorance; he recognizes this in all humility, and is making every effort to remedy it by the application of highly scientific methods. He shares it, moreover, with the representatives of all the social sciences who attempt to carry their work back into the past. The historian will become more and more interested, I believe, in explaining the immediate present, and fortunately

his sources for the last two or three centuries are infinitely more abundant and satisfactory than for the
whole earlier history of the world. He is criticizing
and indexing his sources and rendering them available
to an extent which would astonish a layman unfamiliar
with the tremendous amount that has been accomplished in this respect during the past fifty years.

We have now seethed the kid in its mother's milk.
We have explained history by means of history.
The historian, from a narrow, scientific point of view,
is a little higher than a man of letters and a good deal
lower than an astronomer or a biologist. He need not,
however, repudiate his literary associations, for they
are eminently respectable, but he will aspire hereafter
to find out, not only exactly how things have been, but
how they have come about. He will remain the
critic and guide of the social sciences whose results he
must synthesize and test by the actual life of mankind
as it appears in the past. His task is so fascinating
and so comprehensive that it will doubtless gradually
absorb his whole energies and wean him in time from
literature, for no poet or dramatist ever set before
himself a nobler or a more inspiring ideal, or one
making more demands upon the imagination and
resources of expression, than the destiny which is
becoming clearer and clearer to the historian.

THE NEW ALLIES OF HISTORY

I

THAT history must from time to time be rewritten is an oft-repeated commonplace. Why is this? The past, as ordinarily conceived, seems fixed and settled enough. No theologian has ever conceded to omnipotence itself the power to change it. Why may it not then be described for good and all by any one who has the available information at his disposal? The historian would answer that more and more is being learned about the past as time goes on, that old errors are constantly being detected and rectified and new points of view discovered, so that the older accounts of events and conditions tend to be superseded by better and more accurate ones. This is obvious; but granting that each new generation of historians do their duty in correcting the mistakes of their predecessors, is that all that is necessary? Is there not danger that they will allow themselves to be too largely guided in the choice of their material and in their judgments of it by the examples set by preceding writers? Are historians now adjusting themselves as promptly as they should to the unprecedented amount of new knowledge in regard to mankind in general which has been accumulating during the past generation, and to the fundamental change of attitude that is taking place in our views of man and society?

The usual training which a historical student receives has a tendency to give him the impression that history is a far more fixed and definite thing than it really is. He is aware that various elaborate attempts have been made to establish the *Begriff und Wesen* of history, that its methodology has been the theme of a number of treatises, and that its supposed boundaries have been jealously defended from the dreaded encroachments of rival sciences. Moreover, he finds the general spirit and content of historical works pretty uniform, and he is to be forgiven for inferring that he has to do with a tolerably well-defined subject matter which may be investigated according to a clear and prescribed set of rules. I am inclined, however, to think that this attitude of mind is the result of a serious misapprehension which stands in the way of the proper development of historical study. Before proceeding we must therefore stop a moment to consider the vague meaning of the term "history."

In the first place, history has itself a long and varied history, which was sketched briefly in the preceding essay. Its subject matter, its purposes, and its methods have exhibited in the past a wide range of variation which suggest many future possibilities when we once perceive the underlying causes of these changes. It has, as we have seen, somewhat reluc-

tantly and partially adapted itself to the general outlook of successive periods, and as times changed, it
has changed. In the second place, the scope of historical investigation, as actually carried on at the
present day by those who deem themselves historians,
is so wide as to preclude the possibility of bringing
it into any clearly defined category. The historian
may choose, for example, like Gibbon, to extract
from Procopius's "improbable story" of Alaric's
capture of Rome the circumstances which have an
air of probability. He may seek to determine the
prevalence of malaria in ancient Greece, or to decide
whether the humidity of Asia Minor has altered since
the days of Crœsus, or to trace the effects of the issue
of some forty billions of francs of paper money in
France between 1789 and 1800. As for method, a
peculiar training is essential to determine the diver-
gence between a so-called "eolith" and an ordinary
chip of flint which does not owe its form to human
adaptation; and another kind of training is required
to edit a satisfactory edition of Roger Bacon's *Opus
Majus*. A judicious verdict on the originality of
Luther's interpretation of the words *justitia dei*,
in Romans, i. 17, demands antecedent studies which
would be inappropriate if one were seeking the motives
for Bismarck's interest in insurance for the aged and
incapacitated. I think that one may find solace and
intellectual repose in surrendering all attempts to
define history, and in conceding that it is the business

of the historian to find out anything about mankind in the past which he believes to be interesting or important and about which there are sources of information.

Furthermore, history's chances of getting ahead and of doing good are dependent on its refraining from setting itself off as a separate discipline and undertaking to defend itself from the encroachments of seemingly hostile sciences which now and then appear within its territory. To do this is to misapprehend the conditions of scientific advance. No set of investigators can any longer claim exclusive jurisdiction in even the tiniest scientific field, and nothing indeed would be more fatal to them than the successful defense of any such claim. The bounds of all departments of human research and speculation are inherently provisional, indefinite, and fluctuating; moreover, the lines of demarcation are hopelessly interlaced, for real men and the real universe in which they live are so intricate as to defy all attempts even of the most patient and subtle German to establish satisfactorily and permanently the *Begriff und Wesen* of any artificially delimited set of natural phenomena, whether words, thoughts, deeds, forces, animals, plants, or stars. Each so-called science or discipline is ever and always dependent on other sciences and disciplines. It draws its life from them, and to them it owes, consciously or unconsciously, a great part of its chances of progress.

As Professor J. F. Kemp has so graciously said of his own subject, geology, it could not have matured without the aid of those sister sciences which necessarily preceded it. "The great, round world in its entirety cannot be grasped otherwise than with the assistance of physics, mechanics, astronomy, chemistry, zoölogy, and botany." Not only was geology in its earlier growth "based upon the sister sciences, but now progresses with them, leans largely upon them for support, and in return repays its debt by the contributions which it makes to each." The historical student should take a similar attitude toward his own vast field of research. If history is to reach its highest development it must surrender all individualistic aspirations and recognize that it is but one of several ways of studying mankind. It must confess that, like geology, biology, and most other sciences, it is based on sister sciences, that it can only progress with them, must lean largely on them for support, and in return should repay its debt by the contributions which it makes to our general understanding of our species. Whatever history may or may not be, it always concerns itself with man. Would it not then be the height of folly and arrogance for the historian to neglect the various discoveries made about man by those who study him in ways different from those of the traditional student of the past?

In order to understand the present plight of the **historian** we must go back to the middle of the nine-

teenth century, when for the first time history began
clearly to come under the influence of the modern
scientific spirit. Previously, as we have seen, it had
been a branch of literature with distinctly literary
aims, — when it was not suborned in the interest of
theological theories or called upon to stimulate patriotic pride and emulation. But about sixty years ago
a new era in historical investigation opened which has
witnessed achievements of a character to justify in a
measure the complacency in which historians now and
then indulge. The most obvious of these achievements seem to me to be four in number, and the historian owes all of them, if I am not mistaken, largely
to the example and influence of natural science. He
undertook, in the first place, to test and examine his
sources of information far more critically than ever
before, and rejected partially or wholly many authorities upon which his predecessors had relied implicitly.
Secondly, he resolved to tell the truth like a man,
regardless of whose feelings it might hurt. Thirdly,
he began to realize the overwhelming importance of
the inconspicuous, the common, and often obscure
elements in the past; the homely, everyday, and
normal as over against the rare, spectacular, and
romantic, which had engaged the attention of most
earlier writers. Fourthly, he began to spurn supernatural, theological, and anthropocentric explanations,
which had been the stock-in-trade of the philosophers
of history. I do not propose to dwell upon these

achievements, for no one will be inclined to question their fundamental character. They have cost a tremendous amount of labor, and they were the essential preliminaries to any satisfactory progress. Are they, however, more than essential preliminaries? Do they not, on examination, prove to be rather negative in character? To resolve to tell the truth about what you have taken pains to verify according to your best ability; to reckon with the regular and normal rather than with the exceptional and sensational; and to give up appealing to God and the devil as historical explanations, are but preparations for the rewriting of history. They furnish the necessary conditions rather than the program of progress. Moreover, they are by no means all of the necessary conditions. Still further preparations are essential before the historian can hope to understand the past. Professor William I. Thomas well says: —

The general acceptance of an evolutionary point of view of life and the world has already deeply affected psychology, philosophy, morality, education, sociology, and all the sciences dealing with man. This view involves a recognition of the fact that not a single situation in life can be completely understood in its immediate aspects alone. Everything is to be regarded as having an origin and a development, and we cannot afford to overlook the genesis and stages of change. For instance, the psychologist or the neurologist does not at present attempt to understand the working and structure of the human brain through the adult brain alone. He supplements his studies of the adult brain by observations on the workings of the infant mind, or by an examination of the structure of the infant brain. And he goes farther than this from the immediate aspects of the problem — he examines the mental life and the brain of the monkey, the dog, the rat, the fish, the frog, and of every form of life possessing a nervous system, down to those having only a single cell, and at every point he has a chance of catching a suggestion of the meaning of the brain structure and of mind. In the lower orders of brain the structure and meaning are writ large, and by working up from the simpler to the more complex types, and noting the modification of structure and function point by point, the student is finally able to understand the frightfully intricate human organ, or has the best chance of doing so.

It would seem as if this discovery of the incalculable value of genetic reasoning should have come from the historians, but, curiously enough, instead of being the first to appreciate the full significance of historical-mindedness, they left it to be brought forward by the zoölogists, botanists, and geologists. Worse yet, it is safe to say that, although the natural scientists have fully developed it, the historian has hitherto made only occasional use of the discovery, and history is still less rigidly historical than comparative anatomy or social psychology. Even in recent historical works one finds descriptions of events and conditions, which make it clear that the writer has failed to perceive that all things have an origin and a development, that we cannot afford to overlook their genesis and stages of change, "that not a single situation in life can be completely understood in its immediate aspects alone." Of course the historian has long talked of the "rise" and "fall" of empires, the "growth" and "decay" of institutions; he has of late devoted much attention to the development of institutions, and to this extent he adopts a genetic treatment; but none the less there lies back of all his work the long tradition of what we may call the episodal treatment of the past. He is still discovered making the futile attempt to describe *wie es eigentlich gewesen* without knowing *wie es eigentlich geworden.* The popular misunderstanding of the French Revolution, for instance, is due to the anxiety of the historian to depict the striking events from 1789 onward rather than to interpret them in the light of their antecedents, which are commonly dispatched in an introductory chapter which furnishes no sufficient clue to what follows. The "Renaissance" has been pretty completely misconceived, owing to the ignorance of Burckhardt and Symonds in regard to the previous period. The culture of the Middle Ages in turn remains a mystery to one who has not scrupulously studied the *Weltanschauung* of the fourth century.

The historian still puts himself in the position of one who should wake up in a strange bed and hope to comprehend his situation by taking a careful inventory of the furniture of his room. The strangeness can only be dispelled and the situation understood by falling back on the past — in this case a simple historical consideration such as that one had,

on his way from Chicago to San Francisco, been delayed and obliged to spend the night in Ogden.
Should the historian give us, for instance, the most
minute description of the conditions in the village of
Salem in the year 1692, telling us just where Goody
Bishop's cellar walls stood in which the fatal "pop-
pets" were found, and pointing out the spot where
Nehemiah Abbot's ox met an untimely and suspicious end by choking on a turnip, we should still
fail to grasp this lamentable crisis in the affairs of
New England, for the really vital question is, Why
did our godly ancestors hang old women for alleged
commerce with the devil? Only some knowledge
of comparative religions and of the history of the
Christian church can make that plain. Cotton
Mather was the victim of a complex of squalid superstitions which the Protestant reformers had done
nothing whatever to reduce or attenuate.[1] He is not
to be understood by even the most prayerful study
of his immediate surroundings.

The modern historical student's tendency to specialization, his aspiration to master some single field,
often stands in the way of his really understanding
even what he seems to know most about. The
difference between the best historical writing, which
is rare enough, and the ordinary run of histories, lies
in the historical-mindedness of the author. This is
susceptible of far greater development than it has

[1] See below, pp. 117 *sqq.*

hitherto received,[1] for it should ultimately permeate all historical treatises that pretend to be both constructive and instructive and do not merely confine themselves to the accumulation of the raw material of history.

Historical-mindedness is by no means the only great debt that historians owe to workers in fields seemingly remote from theirs. Two historical facts of transcendent importance were discovered in the latter half of the nineteenth century. Neither of them was in any way attributable to historians. It was the zoölogist who proved that man is sprung from the lower animals, and it was an English geologist who first clearly and systematically brought together the evidence that man has been sojourning on the earth, not for six thousand years only, but mayhap for six hundred thousand. The methods and outlook of the historian prevented him from making these discoveries. He may exonerate himself for his failure to suspect these truths on the ground that the data used to establish man's animal ancestry and his vast antiquity are wholly unfamiliar to him. Granting

---

[1] An interesting paper could be written on the common view entertained by historians that it is impossible to write the history of our own times; that historical methods cannot be applied to recent events. Those who at one moment proclaim this doctrine at the next will freely acknowledge Thucydides, who confined himself to his own time, to be the greatest of all historians ! It is most essential that we should understand our own time; we can only do so through history, and it is the obvious duty of the historian to meet this, his chief obligation.

the propriety of this excuse, it may be asked whether he has seriously reckoned with these two momentous facts after they were pointed out to him by Darwin, Lyell, and others. He has certainly been slow to do so. They were new to the last generation of historians, and they would have seemed quite irrelevant to Ranke or Bancroft in their undertakings. Even to-day I find that members of the guild are some of them inclined to deny that man's descent from the lower animals is, strictly speaking, an historical fact, although they would concede that Henry II's descent from William the Conqueror is such.

What is more important, most historical students would frankly confess that they saw no way in which man's descent or his long sojourn on the earth could be brought into any obvious relation with the problems on which they were engaged. In this they would be quite right. It is certainly true that most historical investigation can be carried on without reference to man's origin. If one is endeavoring to determine whether Charles the Fat was in Ingelheim or Lustnau on July 1, 887, it makes little difference whether the emperor's ancestors talked with their Creator in the cool of the evening or went on all fours and slept in a tree. If one is locating the sites of French forts on the Ohio River or describing the causes of Marie Antoinette's repugnance for Mirabeau, the jaw of the Heidelberg man may safely be neglected. Whole fields of historical research can be cultivated not only

G

without any regard to man's origin, but without any attempt to understand man as such. But there are many other, and perhaps even more important, fields, as I trust may become apparent later, in which it is essential that the investigator should know everything that is being found out about man, unless he is willing to run the risk of superficiality and error.[1]

[1] In order to avoid the suspicion that I am misrepresenting the position of what may be called the orthodox historical student I beg to call the reader's attention to an address delivered by Professor George Burton Adams of Yale before the American Historical Association, December 29, 1908. He describes what, for convenience, he calls five hostile movements directed against the methods, results, and ideals of the established political historian. These "attacks" proceed from political science, geography, political economy, sociology, and "folk-psychology." "For more than fifty years," he says, "the historian has had possession of the field and has deemed it his sufficient mission to determine what the fact was, including the immediate conditions that gave it shape. Now he finds himself confronted with numerous groups of aggressive and confident workers in the same field who ask not what was the fact — many of them seem to be comparatively little interested in that — but their constant question is what is the ultimate explanation of history, or, more modestly, what are the forces that determine human events and according to what laws do they act? This is nothing else than a new flaming up of interest in the philosophy, or the science, of history. . . . The emphatic assertion which they all make is that history is the orderly progression of mankind toward a definite end, and that we may know and state the laws which control the actions of men in organized society. This is the one common characteristic of all the groups I have described; and it is of each of them the one most prominent characteristic" (*American Historical Review*, January, 1909). It is the aim of the present essay to put the whole situation in a different light from that in which Professor Adams presents it.

II

While, then, the historian has been busy doing his best to render history scientific, he has, as we have seen, left the students of nature to illustrate to the full the advantages of historical-mindedness and to make two discoveries about mankind infinitely more revolutionary than all that Giesebrecht, Waitz, Martin, or Hodgkin ever found out about the past. To-day, he has obviously not only to adjust himself as fast as he can to these new elements in the general intellectual situation, but he must decide what shall be his attitude toward a considerable number of newer sciences of man which, by freely applying the evolutionary theory, have progressed marvelously and are now in a position to rectify many of the commonly accepted conclusions of the historian and to disabuse his mind of many ancient misapprehensions. By the newer sciences of man I mean, first and foremost, Anthropology, in a comprehensive sense, Prehistoric archæology, Social and Animal psychology, and the Comparative study of religions. Political economy has already had its effects on history, and as for Sociology, it seems to me a highly important point of view rather than a body of discoveries about mankind. These newer social sciences, each studying man in its own particular way, have entirely changed the meaning of many terms which the historian has been accustomed to use in senses now discredited —

such words as "race," "religion," "progress," "the ancients," "culture," and "human nature." They have vitiated many of the cherished conclusions of mere historians and have served to explain historical phenomena which the historian could by no possibility have rightly interpreted with the means at his disposal. Let us begin with prehistoric archæology.

The conservative historian might be tempted to object at the start that however important the development of man would seem to be before the opening of history, we can unfortunately know practically nothing about it, owing to the almost total lack of documents and records. Archæology has, of course, he would admit, revealed a few examples of man's handiwork which may greatly antedate the earliest finds in Egyptian tombs; some skulls and bones and even skeletons have been found, and no one familiar with the facts doubts that man was living on the earth thousands of years before the Egyptian civilization developed. But what can be known about him, except the shape of his jaw and the nature of his stone and bone utensils, which alone survive from remote periods? If we feel ill-informed about the time of Diocletian or Clovis, how baseless must be our conjectures in regard to the habits of the cave man!

It is certainly true that the home life of the cave man is still veiled in obscurity and is likely to remain so. Nevertheless, the mass of information in regard to mankind before the appearance of the earliest surviving inscriptions has already assumed imposing proportions. Its importance is perhaps partially disguised by the unfortunate old term "prehistoric." The historian glances at case after case of flint eoliths, fist hatchets, arrow points, and scrapers, pictures of animals scratched on bits of bone, fragments of neolithic pottery and bronze "celts," with emotions of weariness tempered by some slight contempt for those who see anything more in these things than the proofs that there used to be savages long ago similar to those that may still be found in regions remote from civilization. Further reflection should, however, convince him that the distinction between "historic" and "prehistoric" is after all an arbitrary one. "Prehistoric" originally meant such information as we had about man before his story was taken up by Moses and Homer, when they were deemed the earliest surviving written sources.

History, however, in the fullest sense of the term, includes all that we know of the past of mankind, regardless of the nature of our sources of information. Archæological sources, to which the student of the earlier history of man is confined, are not only frequently superior in authenticity to many written documents, but they continue to have the greatest importance after the appearance of inscriptions and books. We now accept as historical a great many things which are recorded neither in inscriptions nor in books. It is an historical, not a prehistorical, fact that the earliest well-defined and unmistakable human tool, the fist hatchet, was used in southern Europe, in Africa, India, Japan, and North America. This is exactly as historical as the recorded word that Julius Cæsar first crossed the English Channel at the full of the moon — and far more important.

Should the historical student still find himself indifferent to what has been called palethnology,[1] let him recollect that if, as it is not hazardous to assume, the oldest fist hatchets were made by men living two hundred thousand years ago, the so-called "historical" period of from five to seven thousand years has to do with but a thirtieth or a fortieth of the time man has been slowly and intermittently establishing the foundations of our present civilization. But the fist hatchet is, comparatively speaking, a highly perfected implement and is pretty well diffused over the globe, so that it suggests a vista of antecedent progress which separates man's speechless and toolless ancestors from the makers of the fist hatchets. It must be clear that if one ignores palethnology, one runs the risk of missing the whole perspective of *modern* change. We have outgrown the scale which served for Archbishop Usher,

[1] The term "prehistoric" and some such term as palethnology (suggested by de Mortillet) are still convenient, since the attempt to trace the stages of development of man previous to the appearance of the higher, and really very recent, forms of civilization which first meet us in Egypt and Babylonia involves a particular technical equipment, including, for instance, some acquaintance with geology and paleontology.

who maintained that man and all the terrestrial animals were created on Friday, October 28, 4004 B.C., and which has led to a great deal of shallow talk about our relation to "the ancients" who are in reality our contemporaries.

It seems quite possible — to suggest a single reflection — that human mental capacity has neither increased nor declined during the trifling period which separates us from Plato and Aristotle. Indeed, could we imagine a colony of infants from the first families of Athens in the fifth century B.C., and another the offspring of the most intellectual classes of to-day, completely isolated from civilization and suckled by wolves or fed by ravens, both groups would start in a stage of decivilization suggesting that of the chimpanzee. No one can tell how long it would take the supreme geniuses which such colonies might from time to time produce, to frame a sentence, build a fire, or chip a nodule of flint into a fist hatchet. Nor is there reason to think that either colony would have an advantage over the other in making the first steps in progress. It is only education and social environment that separate the best of us from a savagery far lower than any to be observed on the earth to-day, lower probably than that of the lowest man of whom any traces still exist.

Then there is the word "race," which historical writers have used and still use with great recklessness. Most of the earlier theories of "races" and of the origin of man in western Asia were either consciously suggested, or unconsciously reënforced, by the account in Genesis of the Garden of Eden, the Deluge, and the confounding of language during the construction of the Tower of Babel.   The Aryan theory set forth, for example, by Mommsen in the opening chapter of his *Roman History*, to-day appears well-nigh as naïve and grotesque as the earlier notion of the Tower of Babel. Since the geological period when man may first have made his appearance on the earth, there have been vast changes in the distribution of land and water, in climate and fauna.   These natural changes in physical conditions must have caused all sorts of migrations and fusions; add to these, conquests and invasions, slavery and miscellaneous sexual relations.   These have brought the most varied peoples together and produced an inextricable confusion of morals, manners, and tongues.   In spite of this, one still finds historical students talking of "races" as if we could still believe Max Müller's persuasive tale of the plain of Iran and the dispersion of the Aryans.

These illustrations should be sufficient to substantiate the importance of prehistoric archæology for all students of history, since they all run grave risks of persisting in ancient error if they neglect its results. We are, however, by no means confined to the remains of man and his handiwork for our notions of what must have lain back of the highly developed civilizations which we meet when written records first become available. If, as Professor William Thomas has so happily phrased it, "tribal society is virtually delayed civilization, and the savages are a sort of contemporaneous ancestry," those investigators — namely, the anthropologists — who deal with the habits, customs, institutions, languages, and beliefs of primitive man are in a position to make the greatest contributions to the real understanding of history. From the standpoint of man's development, anthropology may be regarded as a branch of history in the same sense that animal psychology or comparative anatomy are branches of human psychology and human anatomy.

At least one historian of repute has recognized the truth of this. Professor Eduard Meyer prefaces the second greatly revised edition of his *History of Antiquity* with a whole volume of 250 pages on the "Elements of Anthropology." He says: "To have prefaced my work with such an introduction would formerly have excited the surprise and encountered the criticism of many of my judges at a time when the interests of most historians were entirely alien to such questions. Now, when such matters are the order of the day, no apology is necessary. . . . Indeed, such an introduction is absolutely essential for a scientific and consistently conceived history of antiquity."

The helpfulness of anthropology for the historical student is, however, still much obscured, owing partly to his indifference to the whole question of human development, and partly to a more or less justifiable

suspicion on his part that there is grave danger of being
misled in our attempt to interpret past events and
conditions by anthropological theories and schematism.

It is one thing, however, to reject a tool because we
are too stupid to see its use, and another to be on our
guard against cutting ourselves. Even the historical
student who is stolidly and complacently engaged in
determining past facts (except when he puts on the
armor of the Lord to defend the lawful frontiers of
history against invaders) would surely find the study
of anthropology of value. It would tend to give him
poise and insight, preëminently in all matters having
to do with religion or religious sanction, or the underlying forces of conservatism, — and with these subjects
he is constantly engaged in one form or another. No
branch of modern research, indeed, has so upset older
historical conceptions as the comparative study of
religions, a science which is quasi-historical and quasi-
anthropological in its sources and methods. The
older historians failed to see very deeply into religious phenomena; manifestations of that class were
commonly taken for granted, and their origins excited
little curiosity. Yet few phases of human development have proved to be more explicable than the religious. The complex syncretism which resulted in
orthodox Christianity has been laid bare, as well as
the very ancient and primitive superstitions which
were incorporated into the theology of the church
fathers.

I have been told by M. Solomon Reinach, the distinguished director of the Museum of St. Germain-en-Laye, that when Mommsen visited the collections some years ago, he had never heard either of the ice age or of totemism! He appeared to think that the terms might be the ingenious discoveries of M. Reinach himself. Now, Mommsen is properly ranked among the most extraordinary historians of modern times. The mass of his work and its quality are familiar to us all. Nevertheless, his ignorance of two of the commonplaces of prehistoric archæology and anthropology prevented him from seeing the Roman civilization in its proper perspective and from thoroughly grasping its religious, and perhaps even the legal, phenomena. Man, as Henry Adams has so neatly expressed it, is now viewed as a "function" of the ice age during a very long period. As for totemism, it has been called upon to explain such different phenomena as the frescoes in the dark caves of the Magdalénien period, the abhorrence of the Jew for pork, and the esteem of a baseball team for its mascot. Many beliefs and practices of the Christian church are now seen to go back by direct or devious ways to totemism, animism, and the mana.

The historical student who realizes this will hasten to acquaint himself, if he has not already done so, with some of the most suggestive works in this field of anthropology and comparative religion. He will be a very dull person indeed if he does not find his con-

ceptions of the past fundamentally changing as he
reads, let us say, the extracts which Professor Thomas
has so conveniently brought together in his *Source
Book for Social Origins*, or the fascinating *Folkways*,
of the late Professor Sumner; or Solomon Reinach's
Orpheus, Conybeare's *Myth, Magic, and Morals*, or De
Morgan's *Les premières civilisations*, — to mention only
the more obvious examples of this class of literature.

III

So it has come about that the older notions of our
relations to the so-called "ancients," of religion in general and Christianity in particular, and of "race," are
being gravely modified by the investigations of those
who are not commonly classed as historians. These
latter have demonstrated the superficial character of
the older historians' reasoning and pointed the way
to new and truer interpretations of past events and
conditions. Other terms which historians have used
without any adequate understanding of them are
"progress" and "decline," "human nature," "historical continuity," and "civilization." Even a slight
tincture of anthropology, reënforced by the elements
of the newer allied branches of social and animal
psychology, will do much to deepen and rectify the
sense in which we use these terms.

Social psychology, as yet in an inchoate condition,
is based on the conviction that we owe our own ego

to our association with others; it is a social product.
Without others we should never be ourselves. As
Professor George H. Mead expresses it: "Whatever
may be the metaphysical impossibilities or possibilities of solipsism, psychologically it is non-existent.
There must be other selves if one's own is to exist.
Psychological analysis, retrospection, and the study
of children and primitive people give no inkling of
situations in which self could have existed in consciousness except as the counterpart of other selves."

It may at first sight seem a far cry from the origin
of the ego and its dependence on the *socius* to such historical questions as the dates of Sargon's reign, the
meaning of the Renaissance, or Napoleon's views of
the feasibility of invading England. There are, however, plenty of matters of still more vital importance
on which the judgments of historical students are
likely to be gravely affected by some acquaintance
with the recent discussions in regard to the laws of
imitation, with which Tarde's name is especially associated, and with the relation of our reason to the more
primitive instincts which we inherit from our animal
ancestors. Indeed, the great and fundamental question of how mankind learns and disseminates his discoveries and misapprehensions — in short, the whole
rationale of human civilization as distinguished from
the life of the anthropoids — will never be understood
without social psychology; and social psychology
will never be understood without animal psychology;

these studies alone can serve to explain the real nature of progress and retrogression — matters to which no historical student can afford to remain indifferent. There is obviously no possibility of explaining adequately in a brief essay this rather perturbing proposition, but its importance seems to me so great that I am going to venture to present the situation very briefly.

In the first place, is it not clear that we still permit ourselves, as is not at all unnatural, to be victimized by the old anthropocentric conception of things? This has been so long accepted by the western world that in spite of the discoveries of the past sixty years we find many unrevised notions from the past still lurking in the corners of our judgment. We are constantly forgetting, I fear, that man was not created, male and female, in a day, as Mark Hopkins and those of his generation commonly believed. We did not begin our human existence with pure and holy aspirations, a well-developed language, and a knowledge of agriculture, but are descended from a long line of brute ancestors, unable either to talk or to cultivate the soil. All animals that now live or ever have lived on the earth, including man, "are mayhap united together by blood relationship of varying nearness or remoteness." Every one of us has a pedigree stretching back not merely a couple of hundred generations, but through all geologic time since life first commenced on the globe. Man's *bodily* resemblance to the anthropoid apes has long been a subject of comment. Ennius gave expression over two thousand years ago to the disconcerting discovery : —

Simia quam similis, turpissima bestia, nobis ?

With the modern development of zoölogy and comparative anatomy more intimate structural similarities were brought to light; Darwin sketched a portrait of the *turpissima bestia,* our hairy ancestor, with his tail, prehensile foot, and great canine teeth. This hypothesis has since been substantiated by the discovery of numerous vestigial muscles and organs, atavistic reversions, and pathological conditions which can be readily explained only on evolutionary grounds. But if our bodies and their functions so closely resemble those of our nearest relatives among the animals, what shall we say of our minds ? Are these altogether different from the animal minds from which they have gradually developed, or do they perpetuate, like our bodies, all the old that is still available and perhaps not a few traits that now merely hamper us or tend to beget serious disorders ? May not the minds of our remote ancestors, who had not yet learned to talk, still serve us not only in infancy and when senile dementia overtakes us, but may they not be our normal guides in the simpler exigencies of life ? I think that it is not hazardous to affirm that the perpetuation in man of psychological processes to be observed in the other primates would be acknowledged by all students of animal psychology. If this be true, may we not look

to the study of animal psychology, as it develops, for
information which will enable us to discover and appreciate for the first time what really goes to make
up a human being as distinguished from his humbler
relatives?

Comparative, or animal, psychology has only recently found a place in some of our universities.
Professor E. L. Thorndike was perhaps the first, some
twelve years ago, to attempt to put the subject on a
modern experimental basis. Since then much has been
done, especially in the United States. We can hardly
hope to know very clearly what an ape is thinking
about as he looks out from under his wrinkled brow.
"Les animaux ne nous font pas des confidences,"
as Reinach has truly observed. But scientific observation and experimentation are throwing light on
the educability of apes and other animals and on the
ways in which they appear to learn. They have already proved that the chimpanzee can readily master
a vast number of acts over and above anything that
his ancestors have ever known in the jungle. He is
marvelously teachable. He appears to learn by "trial
and error" and by a process which we may term
"trick psychology," stimulated by rewards and punishments. The exact nature and rôle of "imitation"
is not yet very clear, but I think that no one can
doubt its importance. Now the obvious question
forces itself on us, Do we not all learn, for the most
part, much as the chimpanzee learns, by trial and

error and by mastering tricks, stimulated by rewards and punishments, and by "imitation"? The answer will be, I am convinced, that almost all our education is based on modified simian principles. To a believer in the continuity of history that should be a cheering discovery, humiliating as it is in other respects.

I am aware that to most students of history the results of comparative psychology will seem at first sight too remote to have any assignable bearing on the problems that face them. This impression is, however, erroneous, at least where questions of the character and transmission of culture are involved. We cannot understand the nature of culture, as distinguished from our merely animal heritage, without some notion of animal psychology. It seems probable that the historical student will deal far more intelligently with the changes of thought, the development of institutions, the progress of invention, and almost all religious phenomena when he learns to distinguish between the higher and rarer manifestations of peculiarly human psychology and the current and fundamental simian mental modes upon which we still rely so constantly with the assurance of ancestral habit.

I will give but a single illustration from this field of speculation. Gabriel Tarde has emphasized the fact that every minutest element in civilization, every atom of culture that we have, over and above our animal outfit, must either be handed on from one

H

generation to the next, or else be rediscovered, or lost. Now it should be part of the historian's business, and no unimportant part, to follow out the actual historical workings of this rule. Civilization is not innate, but transmitted by "imitation" in the large sense of the word. A word, or a particular form of tool, or a book, will die out as surely as an organism unless it is propagated and regenerated. Let us apply this law in a single case. How little addition to the general disorder and to the chronic discouragements of learning is necessary to account for the fatal disappearance of Greek books in the West after the dissolution of the Roman Empire! Suppose only half as many people in Gaul read Greek in the time of Gregory of Tours as had known it in Constantine's time. How greatly would this increase the chances of the complete disappearance of Xenophon's *Cyropædia* or Euripides's *Elektra*?

In concluding these reflections I am painfully conscious that they may suggest serious dangers to some thoughtful readers. The historical student may be ready to grant that he has neglected the influence that discoveries in other fields should have on his own conclusions; but how, he will ask, is he to find time to acquaint himself with all the branches of anthropology, of sociology, political economy, comparative religion, social psychology, animal psychology, physical geography, climatology, and the rest? It is hard for him even to keep up with the new names, and he has a not unnatural distrust of those who tender him easy explanations for things that they still know so little about. Some of the more exuberant representatives of the newer social sciences remind the historian disagreeably of the now nearly extinct tribe of philosophers of history, who flattered themselves that their penetrating intellects had been able to discover the wherefore of man's past without the trouble of learning much about it.

But the historical student who classes the modern social sciences with the old and discredited philosophy of history is making a serious mistake. The philosophers of history sought to justify man's past in order to satisfy some sentimental craving, and their explanations were, in the last analysis, usually begotten of some theological or national prejudice. The contemporaneous student of society, on the contrary, offers very real and valuable, if obviously partial, explanations of the past. It is true that he sometimes forgets what Hume calls the "vast variety which nature has affected in her operations," and tries to explain more than his favorite cause will account for, but this ought not to blind us to his usefulness.

It is obvious that, like the geologist, the physiologist, and the biologist, the historian is forced to make use of pertinent information furnished by workers in other fields, even if he has no time to master more than the elements of the sciences most nearly allied to his own. He may use anthropological and psychological discoveries and information without becoming either an anthropologist or a psychologist. These discoveries and this information will inevitably suggest new points of view and new interpretations to the historian, and will help to rectify the old misapprehensions and dispel the innumerable ancient illusions which still permeate our historical treatises. Above all, let the historical student become unreservedly historical-minded, avail himself of the genetic explanation of human experience, and free himself from the suspicion that, in spite of his name and assumptions, he is as yet the least historical, in his attitude and methods, of all those who to-day are so eagerly attempting to explain mankind.

It may well be that speculation in the newer fields has often far outrun the data accumulated, and the historical student has not infrequently been offered explanations of the past which he has done well to reject. The sociologist, anthropologist, and economist have doubtless often thought too fast and too recklessly, and this has engendered an excessive reserve in the historian, who has sometimes flattered himself on not thinking at all. But there is, in the long run, more risk in thinking too little than too much, and the kind of thought suggested by the new allies of history should serve, if judiciously practiced, greatly to strengthen and deepen the whole range of historical study and render its results far more valuable than they have hitherto been.

SOME REFLECTIONS ON INTELLECTUAL HISTORY

I

LORD BACON, in his *Advancement of Learning*, says: "No man hath propounded to himself the general state of learning to be described and represented from age to age, as many have done the works of nature and the State civil and ecclesiastical; without which the history of the world seemeth to me to be as the statue of Polyphemus with his eye out; that part being wanting which doth most show the spirit and life of the person. And yet I am not ignorant that in divers particular sciences, as of the jurisconsults, the mathematicians, the rhetoricians, the philosophers, there are set down some small memorials of the schools, authors, and books; and so likewise some barren relations touching the invention of arts or usages. But a just story of learning, containing the antiquities and originals of knowledges and their sects; their inventions, their traditions; their diverse administrations and managings; their flourishings, their oppositions, decays, depressions, oblivions, removes; with the causes and occasions of them, and all other events concerning learning, throughout the ages of the world; I may truly affirm to be wanting."

Three centuries have passed since Bacon wrote these lines, but the deficiency which he points out has not yet been remedied. We have as yet no "just story of learning." It is true that we have histories of certain kinds of thought, especially of philosophy and theology, but these confine themselves in the main to the systems of distinguished thinkers, — the Platos, Aristotles, Kants, and Hegels, the Pauls, Augustines, Aquinases, Luthers, and Jonathan Edwardses, — rather than to the conceptions that were current among their thoughtful contemporaries. Only the simpler and easier portions of a philosophic system can be thoroughly digested by intelligent laymen so as to influence the history of opinion. When we speak of Augustinianism, Hegelianism, or Marxism, we do not mean the complete philosophic systems of these writers, but such particularly impressive discoveries, few in number, as stand out in relief against the mass of subtleties with which only the expert will be tempted to reckon. A member of the intellectual class to-day, looking back and asking himself whence come those ideas which he himself accepts and which he sees accepted by others about him, will for the most part look in vain in histories of philosophy for answers to his questions. Bacon's reproach is still merited, for no one has as yet, so far as I know, ever clearly conceived of a general history of the chief opinions of the intellectual class.

Yet what more vital has the past to teach us than

the manner in which our convictions on large questions have arisen, developed and changed? We do not, assuredly, owe most of them to painful personal excogitation, but inherit them, along with the institutions and social habits of the land in which we live. The content of a well-stocked mind is the product of tens of thousands of years of accumulation. Many widespread notions could by no possibility have originated in modern times, but have arisen in conditions quite alien to those of the present. We have too often, in consequence, an outworn intellectual equipment for new and unheard-of tasks. Only a study of the vicissitudes of human opinion can make us fully aware of this and enable us to readjust our views so as to adapt them to our present environment. If it be true, as was maintained in an earlier essay, that opinion tends, in the dynamic age in which we live, to lag far behind our changing environment, how can we better discover the anachronisms in our views and in our attitude toward the world than by studying their origin? Is not Bacon right in accusing the historian of presenting us with an image of the past without its great cyclopean eye, which alone reveals its spirit and life?

The eager interest of the public in this neglected field is shown by the long-continued popularity of Dr. Draper's *Intellectual Development*. This work has for years enjoyed a reputation far exceeding its merits. From a modern standpoint the book is deficient in almost every respect, except its effective style and the assurance of its author. Dr. Draper has not seen fit at any point to give the reader the slightest clue to the sources of his information, but it is clear to the critical reader that his impressions were derived from such miscellaneous works as were available in the early sixties, and that his conclusions do not at any point rest upon a conscientious study of first-hand material. His object, he frankly tells us, was to prove two laws, which no one nowadays would believe to be laws at all.[1]

About the same time that Draper's work appeared, Lecky published his *Rise and Influence of Rationalism in Europe*. This is on a very different plane from Draper's volumes. It is the result of careful investigation, and exhibits the characteristic prudence and intellectual poise of the writer. Unhappily, however, it confines itself in the main to the last three centuries of European development, with only such background as seemed essential to make the tale clear.

A third work which has attracted much attention is Andrew D. White's *Warfare of Science and Theology*. This is written with a polemical eagerness begotten perhaps of Ex-President White's own effective participation in the battle. He was aided in his work by scholars who supplied him with a large amount of evidence, which he used with the utmost effect in routing the theologians; but the avowed object of the book

---

[1] See above, p. 64, note.

is to reveal the absurdities of patristic and medieval tradition rather than to present impartially the elements of intellectual history.

Leslie Stephen, in his *English Thought in the Eighteenth Century*, has done much to supplement the histories of eighteenth-century philosophy and literature. A. W. Benn, in his *English Rationalism in the Nineteenth Century*, has traced the growing discontent with that class of opinions which had received a religious sanction. Merz's *History of European Thought in the Nineteenth Century* is perhaps the most scholarly and signal contribution to a general history of the intellectual class that has yet appeared. Some of his chapters furnish excellent illustrations of the profitable character of this line of historical investigation. More recently Henry Osborn Taylor has given us a masterly picture of *The Mediæval Mind*, which is at once sympathetic and critical, and is based upon an assiduous intercourse with the sources. All of these, whatever their merits, are, however, confined to particular periods, if we except Draper's now obsolete volumes, and in none of them would the reader find a general summary of the chief phases through which the European intellect has passed.

Any effort to "propound to one's self the general state of learning to be described from age to age" might seem destined to failure in view of the intricate problems offered by each particular period. Nevertheless it would not be impossible, could one emancipate himself from the traditional presentation of the past, to

present in an orderly way the development of the chief
concomitants of our own particular intellectual heritage, always keeping before one the attitude of mind
and range of knowledge of the intellectual class at
large, rather than that of special investigators and
scholars : its convictions on certain large questions,
its methods of reasoning, its powers of criticism, its
authorities, the sources of information that it has
from time to time cherished, whether human or divine,
the range of its knowledge, and the depth of its ignorance, as judged by what had gone before and what
came after.   Special emphasis should naturally be laid
throughout on the modes of attaining and transmitting
knowledge — or what was mistaken for such — and its
application to the welfare and improvement of man's
estate in this world or the next.

II

One who attempted to trace the general history of
thought to-day would have to take into consideration
certain vital discoveries which could not have influenced Lecky and Draper.   We are now tolerably well
assured that could the human mind be followed back,
it would be found to merge into the animal mind, and
that consequently the recently developing study of animal or comparative psychology is likely to cast a great
deal of light upon certain modes of thought.   I do
not mean by this that there is any reason to suppose

that the animals exercise reason in the narrower sense of that term, but that there is, at certain points, a striking parallelism between the methods of learning in the higher animals and in ourselves. In any case a study of animal psychology brings out more clearly than can otherwise be done the essential peculiarities of human psychology. Certain of the higher animals, especially the apes, are remarkably educable and show the possibilities of learning, independently of reason. This capacity for *learning without the use of reason* we not only share with the animals, but we have it in a far greater degree than they. The exact nature of human culture and its method of transmission, as well as of human reason as over against simian mental processes, can only be made apparent by this new science of animal psychology, which is now being assiduously cultivated, especially in the United States. The equally new branch of social psychology, as was pointed out in the previous essay, ought in time to make plainer the nature and extent of our dependence on our fellow-men. In short, we not only retain our animal mind, but, in addition, those more primitive forms of reasoning, which anthropological research is discovering to be common to all so-called primitive peoples. Just as our animal mind stands us in good stead in certain crises, so the more primitive forms of reasoning are always present when they are not submerged by accumulations of knowledge and artificially developed criticism.

Of the gradual clarification of man's psychology through hundreds of thousands of years, we can only judge from the vestiges we have of human handiwork supplemented by the inferences that may be made from the reasoning of the savage and the progressive unfolding of the infant's mind. Previous to the appearance of written records, we must judge of what man *knew*, by the scanty vestiges of what he *did*; in no other way can we discover the foundations of the first historic culture of which we have any tolerable knowledge, that of the Egyptians, dating back five or six thousand years.

The Egyptians do not appear to have led an intellectual life in the later Greek sense of the term. They elaborated an intricate theory of existence after death ; they made many industrial discoveries, and observed the heavens with such care as was necessary in order best to utilize the rise and fall of the river upon which they were dependent for subsistence. Western Europe doubtless owed to the Egyptians more than can ever be determined. It is, however, from the Babylonians and Assyrians that we get our divisions of time, the hours, minutes, and seconds, and the plan of dividing the circle into 360 parts. The Greeks, and, later, western Europe, derived their astrological enthusiasm from these older civilizations.

Intellectual life in the narrower sense of the term appears, as far as we can trace it, to have found its first home among the Ionian Greeks, and especially in the city of Miletus, some six or seven hundred years before Christ. But underlying the speculations of Thales, Anaximander, and other members of this group is the vast substructure which has been touched upon above. When the Ionian philosophers asked what was the *principle* of all things, they asked a question which is highly sophisticated and artificial and which represents a type of scientific abstraction which can only come with great maturity of thought. There has been, so to speak, a desperate struggle ever since the time of Thales to maintain this scientific ambition, which has constantly been threatened with destruction by older and more primitive types of thought, that may be classified as practical, mystical, and romantic.

The Ionian philosophers and those of Elia appear to have exercised their minds on highly metaphysical questions, such as "the one and the many," "being and not being," and the paradoxes which such conceptions suggested. Suddenly, almost without warning, we find the Sophists of Athens presenting a fullness and maturity of intellectual life which in many respects can scarcely be paralleled to-day. Unhappily their works are for the most part lost, and it may well have been that much of their speculation was — like that of Socrates — not written out, but was confined to conversation and oral disputation. Our impressions of what they talked about are derived chiefly from a hostile Plato and from citations in Aristotle.

So abounding is the intellectual vitality of these two

writers, so inexhaustible the range of their speculations, so profound their philosophical penetration, that one who dedicates himself to the study of their works is apt to feel that all intellectual history since their day is only the record of a degeneration. It would become necessary, therefore, in tracing the intellectual history of Europe, to ask one's self not so much what Plato and Aristotle themselves may have believed or discovered, as what particular phases of their thought were generally current among the intellectual class in their own or in later times. It was their fate to become, above all other individual thinkers, the teachers of the Europe from which we derive our intellectual heritage. It must be remembered that, on the one hand, Cicero and the new Academy traced its amiable skepticism back to Plato, and that, on the other hand, Plotinus and the Neoplatonists believed that they derived their super-rational and ecstatic tenets from the same source. As for Aristotle, while he fills the modern critic, whether his interests be in letters, philosophy, science, or politics, with astonishment and admiration, it should not be forgotten that he was the idol of the thirteenth-century scholastics, who made his vicious theory of essences and final causes and his infertile syllogistic reasoning the basis of their speculation.

The scholars of the Hellenistic period at Alexandria and elsewhere appear in certain fields to have carried on the Hellenic traditions in a profitable way, but their additions to knowledge were more than counterbalanced by a vast literature of comment, exegesis, and literary criticism which made little appeal to thoughtful men in the Roman period. The works of the Alexandrian school were mainly permitted to perish, with the notable exception of Euclid and the geographical, astronomical, and astrological compilations of Ptolemy, which were taken up by the Arab scholars and reappeared in the thirteenth century in western Europe.

The melancholy decline of Hellenism in the later Roman Empire was accompanied by the development of new types of intellectual enthusiasm based upon entirely different presuppositions in regard to man's origin and chief business in life. One of the great modern historical discoveries is that what we term "medieval" thought was to all intents and purposes completely elaborated in the later Roman Empire, before the Germans disrupted the western portions of the vast commonwealth organized by Augustus. An emotional revolution had begun as early as Plutarch and had gradually served to denature the traditions of the intellectual life as they had come down from Athens. Reason became an object of suspicion; its impotence seemed to have been clearly proved; the intellectual class sought solace not so much in the restraints of Stoicism as in the *abandon* of Neoplatonism, and the vagaries of theurgy and of oriental mysticism. The clarity and moderation which we associate with Hellenism gave place to the deprecation of reason and a corresponding confidence in the supernatural. Plotinus maintained that only the meaner things of life come within the scope of reason; that the highest truth is supernatural; that it is through intuition rather than reason that we may hope to approach our highest aspirations.

Harnack has well said that Neoplatonism, however lofty and inspiring in some of its aspects, implied nothing less than intellectual bankruptcy. "The contempt for reason and science (for these are contemned when relegated to a second place) finally leads to barbarism, because it results in crass superstition, and is exposed to all manner of imposture. And, as a matter of fact, barbarism succeeded the flourishing period of Neoplatonism. . . . The masses grew up in superstition, and the Christian Church, which entered on the inheritance of Neoplatonism, was compelled to reckon with this and come to terms with it. Just when the bankruptcy of the ancient civilization and its lapse into barbarism could not have failed to reveal themselves, a kindly destiny placed on the stage of European history certain barbarian nations, for whom the work of a thousand years had as yet no existence. Thus the fact is obscured, though it does not escape the eye of one who looks below the surface, that the ancient world must necessarily have degenerated into barbarism of its own accord, because of its renunciation of this world. There was no longer any desire either to enjoy it, to master it, or to know it as it really is. A new world had been disclosed for

which everything in this world was to be given up, and
men were ready to sacrifice insight and understanding,
in order to possess that other world with certainty.
In the light which radiated from the world to come,
that which in this world appeared absurd became
wisdom, and wisdom became folly." [1]

It was just at this period that historical Christianity
received its formulation in the works of the church
fathers. It is suggestive that the greatest of these,
Augustine, had been attracted both by the teachings
of the Persian, Manes, and by the seductions of Neoplatonism. The "Christian Epic," as Santayana has
happily termed it, formed the basis for a new intellectual life which developed in an emotional *milieu* as
different as possible from that of Athens in the fifth
century before Christ. The new thought was able
to take up certain ideal and mystic elements which
may clearly be perceived in Plato, but it had no taste
for the promising contributions to an exact knowledge
of the world which had been made by Democritus and
the Epicureans, who accepted his mechanistic view of
the universe, by Aristotle in his recorded observations,
and by those scientists of the Alexandrian period, such
as Aristarchus, Hipparchus, and Archimedes, who
might, had their spirit and methods prevailed, have
earlier developed that natural science which is the boast
of our own day. The intellectual life as it had been
lived in all its freshness by the contemporaries of

[1] *History of Dogma*, Vol. I, pp. 337-338.

I

Socrates was bound to result eventually in disappointment. It was too exclusively intellectual; it sought truth in purely intellectual operations and clarification. It rarely touched concretely upon the social and economic problems which oppress us to-day, and it failed to recognize the significance of painstaking scientific research or to perceive the possibility of applying the resulting knowledge of the natural world, organic and inorganic, to practical ends.

In this respect the scholastic revival of the twelfth and thirteenth centuries is characteristically Hellenic in spirit. It is true that by that time *authority* was assigned an overwhelming importance, whereas the Athenians, previous to Aristotle's time, had been almost free from this embarrassment. Thomas Aquinas operated with different materials from Plato and gave his thought a different form, but the general intellectual affinity between the two men is apparent enough.

By the end of the twelfth century the first universities were established. Theology became a subject of systematic instruction based upon the convenient outline of patristic opinion furnished by Peter Lombard's *Sentences*. With the reintroduction of Aristotle's works in a defective Latin translation, the older study of the Seven Liberal Arts in the meager epitomes which had come down from earlier centuries was replaced by lectures on all the chief works of the most masterly exponent of Greek thought. If we exclude law and medicine, the two great preoccupations of

the intellectual class in western Europe in the thirteenth century were, accordingly, the highly elaborated
Christian theology, in all its subtle ramifications, on
the one hand, and, on the other, Aristotle's logical
treatises, his *Ethics, Physics, Metaphysics, De Anima*,
and the minor works on natural phenomena, as they
were understood by the ecclesiastical commentators of
the time. With their own observations the schoolmen
combined those of the Arabic philosophers, who had
known and studied Aristotle, above all of Averroes.
The Arabs were, however, rather more remote from
the real Aristotle than Albertus Magnus and Thomas
Aquinas, for their Arabic translations had passed
through Syriac on the way from the Greek. So, as
Renan humorously says of Averroes' commentary,
the western universities prayerfully studied for centuries a Latin translation, of a Hebrew translation,
of an Arabic commentator on an Arabic translation,
of a Syriac translation of a Greek philosopher. Even
supposing that the Latin translations of Aristotle were
as perfect as translations can be, there was little chance
that the thirteenth-century thinker could possibly
transcend all the obstacles that lay in the way of
understanding a Greek philosopher of the fourth
century before Christ. The revival of Aristotle,
instead of rectifying the deficient perspective of the
earlier Middle Ages and supplying knowledge which
would serve as a starting-point for further progress,
only added one more obstacle to a fundamental

readjustment of thought. It enhanced rather than weakened the respect for authority, discouraged rather than promoted the search for fresh truth.

During the fifteenth century Greek was once more revived in Italy. The language had nearly died out in the West about the year 500, and Boethius had made an unsuccessful attempt to perpetuate a knowledge of the chief Greek writers by translating them into Latin, since obviously all knowledge of Greek works was bound to vanish so soon as the knowledge of the language formerly possessed by educated Romans disappeared. For several centuries before Chrysolorus began to teach Greek to a group of eager disciples in Florence in 1396, we find few allusions to Greek works. While the names of Homer and Plato were not forgotten, the scholars of the twelfth century rarely knew of the existence of Æschylus or Sophocles, of Herodotus or Thucydides. The Humanists of the fifteenth century devoted themselves to rediscovering every vestige of Greek literature that could be found, as well as such Latin writers as Tacitus and Lucretius, who had been forgotten. They translated the Greek books into Latin, and thus rendered current in intellectual circles those works that still remain to us from classical antiquity.

It is, however, a grave mistake to assume that this renewed interest in the Greek and Roman authors betokened a revival of Hellenism, as has commonly been supposed. The libraries described by Vespasiano, a

Florentine bookseller of the fifteenth century, indicate the least possible discrimination on the part of his patrons. Ficino, the translator of Plato, was an enthusiastic Neoplatonist, and to Pico della Mirandola the Jewish Cabbala seemed to promise infinite enlightenment. In short, *Plato was as incapable in the fifteenth century of producing an intellectual revolution as Aristotle had been in the thirteenth.* With the exception of Valla, whose critical powers were perhaps slightly stimulated by acquaintance with the classics, it must be confessed that there was little in the so-called "New Learning" to generate anything approaching an era of criticism. It is difficult, to be sure, to imagine a Macchiavelli or an Erasmus in the thirteenth century, but it is likewise difficult to determine the numerous and subtle changes which made them possible at the opening of the sixteenth; and it is reckless to assume that the Humanists were chiefly responsible for these changes.

The defection of the Protestants from the Roman Catholic Church is not connected with any decisive intellectual revision. Such ardent emphasis has been constantly placed upon the differences between Protestantism and Catholicism by representatives of both parties that the close intellectual resemblance of the two systems, indeed their identity in nine parts out of ten, has tended to escape us. The early Protestants, of course, accepted, as did the Catholics, the whole patristic outlook on the world; their historical perspective was similar, their notions of the origin of man, of the Bible, with its types, prophecies, and miracles, of heaven and hell, of demons and angels, are all identical. To the early Protestants, as to Catholics, he who would be saved must accept the doctrine of the triune God and must be ever on his guard against the whisperings of reason and the innovations suggested by scientific advance. Luther and Melanchthon denounced Copernicus in the name of the Bible. Melanchthon re-edited, with enthusiastic approval, Ptolemy's astrology. Luther made repeated and bitter attacks upon reason; in whose eyes he freely confessed the presuppositions of Christianity to be absurd. Calvin gloried in man's initial and inherent moral impotency; and the doctrine of predestination seemed calculated to paralyze all human effort.

The Protestants did not know any more about nature than their Catholic enemies; they were just as completely victimized by the demonology of Witchcraft. The Protestant Revolt was not begotten of added scientific knowledge, nor did it owe its success to any considerable confidence in criticism. As Gibbon pointed out, the loss of one conspicuous mystery — that of transubstantiation — "was amply compensated by the stupendous doctrines of original sin, redemption, faith, grace, and predestination" which the Protestants strained from the epistles of St. Paul. Early Protestantism is, from an intellectual standpoint, essentially a phase of medieval religious history.

III

Before the end of the sixteenth century, however, Montaigne reveals an unmistakable Hellenic urbanity, which awakens one to the deficiencies and disappointments of the so-called Renaissance. He does not rise to the mystic heights of Plato, but vies with him in his complete freedom from dogma and authority, and in the tentativeness and humanity of his conclusions.

At last, with the opening of the seventeenth century, the beginnings of that intellectual revolution which is carrying us far beyond the limits of Greek thought are clearly apparent. To one man in especial we owe the first statement of the main aspects of the change. Lord Bacon, in his *Advancement of Learning*, and later in his *Organon*, discusses with great acumen the obstacles which lie in the way of progress, and the methods of overcoming them. He saw far more clearly than any of his contemporaries, or, at any rate, expressed in a far more effective way, the prospects of scientific discovery and its application to the betterment of man's estate. He analyzed the nature of authority and pointed out its dangers. He foresaw an infinite vista of possibilities in the accumulation of new knowledge about man and the world through experimental scientific research. In his ideal commonwealth, the New Atlantis, he provides an academy of science to which he assigns the most prominent place, and he dwells at great length upon its elaborate equipment.

To him knowledge was above all dynamic and pro-gressive, and in his works our modern idea of human progress first appears in unmistakable form. It is quite true that he was not himself destined to make any considerable contribution to natural science, nor did he appreciate the contributions which his con-temporaries, such as Galileo and Harvey, were making. He even refused to accept the Copernican theory of the solar system, and exhibits, moreover, at times a highly naïve reliance upon authority; all of which only proves the great difficulty of making a sudden break with the past, however good one's intentions may be.

Descartes went much farther in his distrust of authority than Bacon.   As is well known, he believed that a complete system of knowledge could be created *de novo*, by observing the methods which he prescribed in the search for truth.   His *Essa de la Methode* is fundamentally a declaration of complete independence of the past and a repudiation of the medieval attitude of mind.   Like Bacon and Galileo, he ventured to write his most profound thoughts in his own native tongue, thus recognizing that the intellectual class was no longer confined to those who had mastered Latin.

Descartes's plan of emptying his mind and starting over again certainly marks an epoch in philosophic thought; but, as might have been anticipated, the moment that he permitted his mind to refill itself, the ideas that poured in were mainly old ones.   Unconsciously, indeed, he merely found a new excuse for reinstalling a great part of his ancient intellectual furniture.   Just as Bacon's new method of reaching truth failed to free him from old errors, so Descartes, in his initial anxiety to prove the existence of God, showed a strongly conservative tendency.   Nevertheless, he and Bacon scotched authority, although they had not the heart to kill it, and the unprecedented intellectual clarification, accompanied by an unprecedented accumulation of facts in regard to man and his environment, which succeeding centuries have witnessed is largely due to the attitude of mind which Bacon and Descartes encouraged.

During the seventeenth century there was a general awakening of a bold, critical spirit which had been unknown in western Europe since the disappearance of the skeptics in the later Roman Empire.   This is particularly conspicuous in matters which had received a religious sanction.   A theory of tolerance was developed by Locke and others; miracles became a stumbling-block; Spinoza outlined a system of higher criticism in dealing with the Old Testament; Pierre Bayle scrutinized somewhat unsympathetically the records of religious heroes, such as David and Augustine; and before the end of the seventeenth century the first chapters of Genesis had become the subjects of playful exegesis in the hands of Dr. Burnet and Charles Blount.   Herbert of Cherbury, in his *Ancient Religion of the Gentiles*, had earlier laid the foundations for the study of comparative religion and protested against the idea that God proposed to damn the greater portion of mankind. Newton's proof that our terrestrial laws of motion extend throughout the universe made a far more profound impression than the writings of Copernicus, and the eighteenth-century Deists never tired of praising a God of immutable law.

The bases of modern astronomy, physics, botany, zoölogy, and mathematics were all laid before the middle of the eighteenth century, and by that time the knowledge in all these subjects greatly transcended, in its extent and precision, anything known to the Greeks and Romans. The diabolical superstitions associated with witchcraft, which, it must be remembered, were based upon the Bible and classical authors, finally gave way, and the new spirit of unfettered criticism and the confidence in experimental science and its applications which it had begotten — which were ever reënforcing the conception of progress and were ever weakening the authority of the past — furnished the necessary preliminaries for a new series of achievements.

IV

This sketch of intellectual history down to the middle of the eighteenth century should put us in a position to reach some general conclusions in regard to the main peculiarities of our present outlook. It is conceded even by the most intrepid Hellenic enthusiasts that, as we compare our own with earlier periods, there can be no doubt that there is a large element of novelty in the present situation.   Nobody questions that in such matter as locomotives, sewing machines, steam threshers, telephones, and arc lights our age is one unparalleled in the past.   There is, however, still a very common feeling, especially among men of the highest degree of literary and artistic cultivation, that our advance beyond the Greeks in art and litera-ture is somewhat questionable, and with this goes the suspicion that the Greeks exhibited practically all the varieties of intellectual activity which we now witness, that here and there they forecast almost all of our fundamental scientific discoveries, and that their ideals of the intellectual life were equal, if not superior, to anything to which man has since attained.

It seems to the writer that this suspicion is the re-sult of a failure to realize certain fundamental novelties which underlie the characteristic thought of our own time.   At least five such novelties appear to be rather easily distinguishable.   Two of them have already been mentioned : (1) Experimental science, which engages in a minute observation of natural phenomena aided by instruments adapted to the purpose, and verified by experimentation, is essentially a product of modern times.   The Greeks had no telescopes, nor microscopes, nor thermometers, nor spectroscopes.   Their knowl-edge was at best the result of what would seem to us crude and haphazard observation which tended to take the form of accepted authority. Why, the Scholastics would have asked, is it necessary to see whether a heavy body falls more rapidly than a light one, since Aristotle has told us that it does? Then in the second place, (2) our modern idea of progress through the continual discovery of new knowledge and the improvement of man's condition is one that does not appear clearly among the Greeks and Romans.

Into the thought of the nineteenth century, three additional elements entered: —

(3) In some inexplicable way there has come a respect for, and appreciation of, the common man, a solicitude for his welfare, and a willingness to permit him to share in the control of public affairs. These together constitute what may be called the democratic spirit. So long as slavery or serfdom existed, as they did down until recent times, the democratic spirit was impossible. It is this appreciation of the common man which is reflected in our development of social sciences, undreamed of by the Greeks, and in the socializing of older subjects, such as psychology and ethics. Political economy was born in the eighteenth century; in the nineteenth anthropology developed on a large scale, together with the comparative study of religions, sociology, and social psychology.

(4) The tendency to occupy this social point of view has been greatly increased by another new factor, the *Industrial Revolution*, with all its attendant circum-

stances. By the Industrial Revolution is, of course, meant the fundamental change in our methods of economic production and organization due to the development of machinery and the factory system. At first sight these matters would seem remote from the life of the intellect. Why should our general view of the world be materially affected by new ways of spinning and weaving and more efficient methods of manufacturing boots and shoes? Simply because it suggests hitherto unsuspected possibilities of social readjustment and the promotion of human happiness, — two of the most engaging subjects of modern speculation. As Robert Owen pointed out, our increased capacity of production through machinery is equivalent to vastly increasing the number of workers in the world without any increase of the number of persons to be cared for. If, in a manufacturing town of twenty thousand inhabitants, modern machinery permits an output which formerly would have required two hundred thousand workers, each individual will have, on the average, nine helpers in providing the necessities and material amenities of life. Hitherto the Industrial Revolution has, from the standpoint of the common man, been distinctly disappointing in its results. For a variety of reasons, which it is impossible to enumerate here, the work done by his helpers appears to profit him very little. Nevertheless, the intellect has perhaps never had a more exhilarating problem set before it than the possibilities of readjustment implied in the economic revolution.

We owe, moreover, to the Industrial Revolution the development of our cities, and city life has always been closely associated with intellectual changes, so that we are justified in assuming that the vast extension of our urban interests must ultimately deeply affect our speculations. Associated with these same economic changes is the development of world-commerce and of incredibly efficient means of communication, which have brought mankind together throughout the whole earth in a spirit of competition, emulation, and co-operation. It will not be many years before every one on the face of the globe can read and write and be in a position through our means of intercommunication to follow the course of events in every portion of the earth. This astonishing condition of affairs suggests boundless possibilities of human brotherhood. A few years ago, at an International Postal Congress, as I recollect, a proposition was made that the charge for a letter between almost any two points on the surface of the globe be reduced to two cents. This was advocated by Egypt, the United States, and New Zealand. This proposition and those who supported it, representing at once the land of the oldest civilization and, on the opposite side of the globe, that of the newest, ought sufficiently to free us from the idea that our speculation can be limited to the bounds which circumscribed that of the Greeks.

(5) Reënforcing all these tendencies is the modern evolutionary view. The discovery, known as evolution, that all things come about gradually and that one thing grows out of another, has perhaps done more than any other new element in our thought to discredit the ways of thinking that prevailed in ancient Greece and among the Schoolmen of the Middle Ages. As Professor John Dewey has pointed out, the very words "Origin of Species" chosen by Darwin as the title of his book, embody a general intellectual revolt against the earlier assumptions, and a new intellectual temper, the full significance of which has hitherto scarcely been realized. The Greek thinkers were not wholly oblivious to the development of the world, but they knew little or nothing about the history of the globe or of mankind, and in general believed in fixed kinds of things, — in distinct and immutable species, — and this belief received the religious sanction of Christian thinkers. It carried with it as a natural corollary "the assumption of the superiority of the fixed and final," and regarded "change and origin as signs of defect and unreality." "In laying hands upon the sacred ark of absolute permanency," Professor Dewey continues, "in treating the forms that had been regarded as types of fixity and perfection as originating and passing away, the *Origin of Species* introduced a mode of thinking that in the end was bound to transform the logic of knowledge, and hence the treatment of morals, politics, and religion." Platonic ideas,

Aristotelian essences, the Christian dogma of special creation, and "eternal verities" in general are involved in the *débâcle*. "The human mind, deliberately as it were, exhausted the logic of the changeless, the final, and the transcendent, before it essayed adventure on the pathless wastes of generation and transformation." But now that it has engaged in this novel adventure its interest inevitably shifts "from the wholesale essence back of special changes to the question of how special changes serve and defeat concrete purposes; shifts from an intelligence that shaped things once for all to the particular intelligences which things are even now shaping; shifts from an ultimate goal of good to the direct increments of justice and happiness that intelligent administration of existent conditions may beget and that present carelessness or stupidity will destroy or forego." [1]

This evolutionary way of thinking is the inevitable result of the highly dynamic age in which we live. Even if it had not been shown by paleontologists, botanists, and zoölogists that the now existing species of plants and animals had developed from preëxisting species, the older philosophic concepts of the Greeks and Schoolmen must have ultimately given way before the general advance of scientific knowledge and the Industrial Revolution. The botanists and zoölogists and the prehistoric archæologists have furnished us

[1] Dewey, John, *The Influence of Darwin on Philosophy and Other Essays in Contemporaneous Thought*, 1910, pp. 1-19.

with an astonishing and satisfying historical example of an evolutionary process, but even without this, the older philosophy based on fixed species and essences, and relying upon Aristotelian logic as an efficient method of attaining truth, was doomed. The discovery of organic evolution was the culmination, not the beginning, of a philosophical revolution.

In view of what has been said, is it not clear that modern thought far transcends that of the Greeks in the accumulation and precision of the data on which it is founded, in the critical and historical methods of treating and interpreting this data, in the rejection of unsound philosophical assumptions and futile antitheses which have proved a serious obstacle in the path of enlightenment, and, lastly, in the ingenious application of knowledge to human needs? It is true that the Alexandrian Greeks received from Aristarchus the suggestion that the earth revolved on its axis and about the sun, from Archimedes and Hero illustrations of important mechanisms, and they knew of the Epicurean theory (later eloquently reproduced by Lucretius) of man's slow development, *but they were incapable of appreciating the importance of any of these suggestions.* As Professor Dewey says, they seemed pledged to exhaust the logic of the changeless, the final, and the transcendent, and consequently their game was bound to be played out sooner or later. But it seems as if our game can scarcely be played to an end. There is no reason to think that we are making more than the

K

earliest discoveries and the crudest applications of
knowledge as yet.   The possibilities of fruitful research
seem unlimited and the influence of new knowledge
incalculable.

We have learned to think about a far wider range of
things than any generation which has preceded us;
we have learned to recognize that truth is not merely
relative, as was clearly enough perceived by an important school of Greek thought, but that this relativity is conditioned by our constant increase in knowledge.   Cicero declared that there was no possible view
that had not been held by some philosopher, and that
it was the part of the wise man to accept the opinion
that appeared to him at the moment the most plausible.   While there is much in Cicero's skepticism to
admire, we should now state our plight in quite different terms.   Our more carefully considered opinions
are based ultimately upon observed facts about man
and his environment.   With our ever increasing
knowledge in regard to these facts, our opinions must
necessarily change.   To what may be called the innate
relativity of things, perceived by the Greeks, we have
added a dynamic relativity which is the result of rapidly advancing scientific knowledge, which necessarily
renders all our conclusions provisional.

In the career of conscious social readjustment upon
which mankind is now embarked, it would seem as if
the history of thought should play a very important
part, for social changes must be accompanied by emo-

tional readjustments and determined by intellectual guidance. The history of thought is one of the most potent means of dissolving the bonds of prejudice and the restraints of routine. It not only enables us to reach a clear perception of our duties and responsibilities by explaining the manner in which existing problems have arisen, but it promotes that intellectual liberty upon which progress fundamentally depends.

HISTORY FOR THE COMMON MAN

I

SHOULD a student of the past be asked what he regarded as the most original and far-reaching discovery of modern times, he might reply with some assurance that it is our growing realization of the fundamental importance and absorbing interest of common men and common things. Our democracy, with all its hopes and aspirations, is based on an appreciation of common men; our science, with all its achievements and prospects, is based on the appreciation of common things. It is impossible to pause here to show how very true this is, nor is it needful to do so, for we all seem to recognize its truth by our presence here to-day to consider the particular problem before us.[1] We have come together with a view of adjusting our education to this great discovery. It is our present business to see what can be done for that very large class of boys and girls who must take up the burden of life prematurely and who must look forward to earning

[1] Read before the superintendents of schools of the larger cities at the meeting of the National Educational Association at Indianapolis, March 2, 1910. The general subject under consideration at this meeting was Industrial Education.

their livelihood by the work of their hands. But education has not been wont until recently to reckon seriously with the common man who must do common things. It has presupposed leisure and freedom from the pressing cares of life.

This conception can be traced back to the Greeks, who established the tradition that education should be "liberal" and based on "liberal arts," by which they meant those studies and that training which they believed appropriate for a freeman who was supported by slaves and who had before him a life of leisure. When a particular study suggested in any way practical usefulness, it lost forthwith its "liberal" character, for it could only be advantageous to a slave. It has proved very difficult to get away from this long-cherished conception of education, for we do not realize vividly enough the changes which have taken place since Aristotle painted his portrait of the "high-minded" man. The Greeks had neither democracy in our sense of the term, nor natural science as we understand it, with its multiform applications to life. Slavery has disappeared, and the ancient occupations of the slave have undergone such a revolution, have been so diversified and shown such possibilities of improvement with the advance of scientific discovery, that modern industry bears little resemblance to the simple handicrafts of earlier times. Industry has become exceedingly interesting and worthy. We have no right to exclude it from our education as the Greeks did. We have no excuse for continuing to harbor their prejudice against the practical, and must not permit ourselves to be dominated any longer by their notion of "liberal" as something which must be kept carefully apart from the "useful." It is high time that we set to work boldly and without any timid reservations to bring our education into the closest possible relation with the actual life and future duties of the great majority of those who fill our public schools.

With this conviction firmly implanted in my mind, I propose to point out the rôle that history may be made to play in the education of boys and girls who are being taught to manage machinery and carry on other industrial operations with the immediate end of supporting themselves. When I first began teaching history, I must admit that I did not see its uses very clearly. This was due largely to the fact that I had a very inadequate notion of what the past of mankind really means for us. I have gradually come to realize how completely we are dependent on the past for our knowledge and our ideals; how it alone can explain why we are what we are, and why we do as we do. History is what we know of the past. We may question it as we question our memory of our own personal acts and experiences. But those things that we recall in our own past vary continually with our moods and preoccupations. We adjust our recollection to our needs and aspirations, and ask from it light on the particular problems that face us.

History, too, is in this sense not fixed and immutable, but ever changing. Each age has a perfect right to select from the annals of mankind those facts that seem to have a particular bearing on the matters it has at heart. And so it comes about, as Maeterlinck has pointed out, that, with increased insight, historic facts "which seemed to be graven forever on the stone and bronze of the past will assume an entirely different aspect, will return to life and leap into movement, bringing vaster and more courageous counsels."

This is a very important point, and I am anxious to emphasize it before I go on, for I have no idea of recommending for industrial schools the particular kind of history that commonly goes by that name, since it is not suitable for our purposes. There are no clearly defined "elements" in the study of history, as there are in arithmetic. Doubtless those who prepare our historical manuals believe that they are including the most important things that have happened, just as a chemist or geologist would present in a textbook the elements of his particular branch of natural science. The case of history is, however, quite peculiar, for it has to do with the most diverse and heterogeneous matters, and not, like chemistry, with a pretty well-defined class of phenomena. Our so-called standard works on history deal at length with kings and popes, with courtiers and statesmen, with wars waged for territory or thrones, with laws passed by princes and parliaments. But these matters form only a very small part of history, for the historian may elect to describe a Roman villa or a primitive steam engine, or contrast the theology of Luther with that of St. Thomas Aquinas; he can trace the origin of Gothic architecture or of the Egyptian calendar, portray the infatuation of Henry VIII for Anne Boleyn, or Bismarck's attitude toward the socialists, or the hatchets of neolithic man. This list of illustrations but feebly suggests the range and inexhaustible variety of man's interests and achievements. Some of these things are usually included in our textbooks, some are not.

What assurance have we that, from the boundless wealth of the past, the most important and pertinent of the experiences of mankind have been sifted out and brought into due prominence by those who popularize history and squeeze it into such compendious forms as they believe best adapted to the instruction of youth? I think that we have no such assurance. Voltaire long ago pronounced history to be simply a tale that we have agreed upon — *une fable convenue.* He is right; each new writer of a textbook is guided, consciously or unconsciously, in his choice of topics by earlier manuals which have established what teachers and the public at large are wont to expect under the caption "history."

Until recently the main thread selected was political. Almost everything was classified under kings' reigns; and the policy of their governments and the wars in which they became involved were the favorite subjects of discussion. This is a venerable tradition established by the Greek and Roman historians, Thucydides, Polybius, Livy, Tacitus. Political history is the easiest kind of history to write; it lends itself to accurate chronological arrangement, just because it deals mainly with events rather than with conditions. It must, moreover, have seemed more important to readers when kings and courts were far more conspicuous than they now are, and when fighting was regarded as the one unmistakably genteel pursuit of the leisure classes. Some writers justified it on the ground that this kind of history served as a guide to generals and statesmen who, by studying the past, might learn better to conduct an army to victory or guide the ship of state in the dangerous waters of civil commotion or foreign aggression.

It is clear that our interests are changing, and consequently the kind of questions that we ask the past to answer. Our most recent manuals venture to leave out some of the traditional facts least appropriate for an elementary review of the past and endeavor to bring their narrative into relation, here and there, with modern needs and demands. But I think that this process of eliminating the old and substituting the new might be carried much farther; that our best manuals are still crowded with facts that are not worth while bringing to the attention of our boys and girls and that they still omit in large measure those things that are best worth telling.

In order to make the situation quite clear, let us imagine that some broad-minded and sympathetic spirit, deeply impressed with the tasks that face us to-day, — like Maeterlinck himself, for instance, — had managed to learn a great deal about the past of mankind without ever looking into a standard history or an historical manual great or small; that he had been guided miraculously to the real sources of historical knowledge and had familiarized himself with all the vestiges of the past thought and activities of mankind, not only the written records, but the remains of buildings, pictures, clothing, tools, and ornaments. Let us suppose, then, that he undertook to prepare a book for children, in which he proposed to tell them what he believed would be most interesting to them, and most illuminating, as they grew up and began to play their respective parts in social life. Would he dream of including the battle of Ægospotami, the Samnite wars, the siege of Numantia by the Romans, the crimes of Nero, the Italian campaigns of Frederick Barbarossa, the six wives of Henry VIII, or the battles of the Thirty Years' War? It is tolerably safe to say that none of these things, which our manuals always include, would even occur to him as he thought over all that man had done and thought and suffered and dreamed through thousands of years.

Our writer, not being especially interested in battles and sieges or the conduct of kings, and having no idea of teaching his readers how to be good generals and statesmen, would in all probability select some other thread for his narrative than the old political one. He might decide that what men knew of the world, or what they believed to be their duty, or what they made with their hands, or the nature and style of their buildings, whether private or public, were far more suggestive to us than their rulers at particular times or the wars that they waged. So in considering the place to be assigned to history in industrial education, I have no intention, as I have already said, of advocating what has hitherto commonly passed for an outline of history. On the contrary, I suggest that we take up the whole problem afresh, freed for the moment from our impressions of "history" vulgarly so-called.

Let us begin by asking ourselves what, considering the needs, capacity, interests, and future career of the boys and girls in industrial schools, is it most necessary for them to know of the past in order to be as intelligent, efficient, and happy as possible in the life they must lead and the work they must do? In order to answer this question intelligently, we must first determine the position in which the pupils are placed, and the nature of the demands which their special kind of education imposes. Secondly, I propose to give some illustrations of those things in the social memory of mankind which are most essential for them to know and recall from time to time, and which I venture to think will prove more enlightening than any other information that can be given them.

II

Industrial education is, of course, a form of technical education. Its most obvious immediate aim is to prepare boys and girls, thirteen to sixteen years old, to become skillful operatives as promptly as may be. With this technical training we are not here concerned. But industrial training may aspire to do much more than turn out efficient artisans who will satisfy their employers, and who will command higher wages and be eligible to a more rapid promotion than the untrained — fundamental as all this is. The industrial class is a very large one indeed, and it is obviously of the greatest moment to society that this class should be recruited from those who have been taught to see the significance of their humble part in carrying on the world's work, to appreciate the possibilities of their position, and to view it in as hopeful a light as circumstances will permit.

Now it must be admitted that the circumstances in which a boy or girl begins and continues work in a modern factory are far from cheerful. They are usually very depressing, physically and mentally. A monotonous repetition of a series of motions continued hour after hour and day after day and year after year, in dingy and noisy surroundings, would seem on the surface to be all that there is of it. As Wyckoff has so truly said, the workmen carry on each his particular process without in the least knowing what it really means; consequently, they can have "no personal pride in its progress, and no community of interest with their employer. There is none of the joy of responsibility, none of the sense of achievement, only the dull monotony of grinding toil, with the longing for the signal to quit work, and for their wages at the end." If this be true, how can the workers be expected to have the least appreciation of the social and industrial value of their labor? How can they be expected to take an intelligent view of their responsibilities, or conceive rational plans for bettering their condition? This is the general situation which those who organize industrial schools must face, fairly and squarely.

In their endeavors to offset the existing evils, I am convinced that they will be forced to summon history to their aid — not the history now to be found in our textbooks, but those phases of past human experience and achievement which serve to explain our industrial life and make its import clear. History alone can explain the existence of the machine which the operative must tend. It is the very last link in a chain of marvelous discoveries reaching back hundreds of thousands of years to the bits of flint which were among man's earliest implements and which may have started him on his long career of mechanical invention and social development. The operative will learn from history how the present division of labor, of which he seems to be the helpless victim, has come about; he will perceive its vast social significance and will comprehend the rather hard terms on which things get made rapidly, cheaply, and in great quantities. An understanding of this may suggest ways in which as he grows older, he can become influential in bettering the lot of himself and his fellows without seriously diminishing the output, and conciliate economic efficiency with the welfare of the workmen, — which is, after all, as important a problem as exists in industrial life.

For example, it seems to an outsider as stupid as it is disastrous that, with the simplification of processes through the division of labor, there has not been a countervailing tendency to enable the workman to carry on in succession a series of contributions to the completed product. The grinding monotony might be relieved, from time to time, by a reasonable alternation of duties so as to bring into play a new set of muscles and of mental adjustments. There are, assuredly, a considerable number of disadvantages in prevailing practices which a more intelligent, sympathetic, and alert set of workmen could coöperate in abolishing or alleviating without serious economic sacrifice.

Besides giving the artisan an idea of social progress and its possibilities, history will furnish him a background of incidental information which he can utilize in his daily surroundings, and which will arouse and foster his imagination by carrying him, in thought, far beyond the narrow confines of his factory. It is impossible to do more than enumerate a few of the most conspicuous and impressive facts in man's development, which would arouse the attention of the boys and girls, and might, as the years went on, give them an outlook on life that they would get in no other way. We might begin with the well-known fact that man is by no means the only artisan in our world. Without his tools, he would be unable to compete with the spider, the bee, or the wasp. Certain birds construct very elaborate dwellings for themselves and their families, but man's ancestors, to judge from his nearest relatives which exist to-day, could do no more than make a rude platform of boughs. When our distant forebears began to walk firmly on their hind legs and thus found their hands free, then it was that their good, big brains began to undergo those changes that make them so superior to those of the highest apes. In this long process we may assume that two factors have been specially potent in developing the peculiarly human heritage of culture, as distinguished from the instinctive and often marvelous skill of other animals : these are language and the invention of tools.

In the beginning, man was a far more clumsy and inefficient artisan than the wasp; but he had the great advantage, if he happened to be particularly clever, of being able, not only to do something from time to time that his ancestors had never done, but to transmit this improvement to succeeding generations. How the wasp developed its skill we do not know; but, as it now is, so it remains — it neither increases nor declines, as does human culture, for the simple reason that it does not have to be taught to each generation by the last. Could we imagine a child to-day growing up absolutely untaught and unaffected by the example of those around him, he would, in all probability, be little superior in point of civilization to a baboon. In short, our achievements are not innate, — we owe practically all of them to past generations. The accumulation of culture and its transmission by education in the widest sense of the word is the chief distinction and duty of our species. A great part of our development, and a great part of the heritage that has been transmitted to us from age to age, is associated with our implements. By his tools man can be traced back through hundreds of thousands of years. Indeed, only the stones and bits of flint that he modified to his uses survive from the very remote periods. The French anthropologists have established a succession of eras in the history of the old stone men, based on the variety and finish of their implements. The history of man, then, begins with his industries; and I am not sure that his industries, in a broad sense of the term, have not always constituted as good a single test of his general civilization and as satisfactory a clue to its vicissitudes as can be found.

After the last advance of the ice sheet in Europe,

and perhaps not more than seven to ten thousand years ago, the so-called "neolithic" phase of civilization clearly emerges, with its ground stone implements, its pottery, agriculture, and domestic animals. This stage, before the gradual introduction of metals, seems to have prevailed very generally in both the old world and the new. It lies back of the civilization of Egypt and Babylonia; it was the condition in which the Europeans found the peoples of America, four centuries ago; and it may still be studied in various parts of the earth where it continues to exist. There should be no difficulty in explaining vividly to a child this intermediate grade of civilization, — so complicated from the standpoint of the chimpanzee, so simple from the standpoint of that of Greece or Rome.

The recent discoveries in Egypt indicate that some four thousand years before Christ a marked advance beyond the neolithic age had already taken place there. A rapid and graceful system of writing had been developed, copper was beginning to be used for vessels, and, when properly hardened, it became available for tools. The ancient Egyptian seems to have been an ever industrious and practical person, to whom business made a strong appeal. The book-keeper is a conspicuous figure in the paintings which have come down to us. The Egyptian's art was closely associated with his peculiar environment and his industries. As Breasted has well said: "The

L

lotus blossomed on the handle of his spoon, and his
wine sparkled in the deep blue calix of the same
flower; the muscular limb of the ox in carved ivory
upheld the couch on which he slept; the ceiling over-
head was a starry heaven resting on palm trunk
columns, each crowned with its graceful tuft of droop-
ing foliage."

The range of Greek manufactures might also easily
be brought into instructive relation with both their
art and their conceptions of life, in such a way as to
give a far more adequate notion of this extraordinary
people than one is likely to derive from the textbooks
that tell of their political assemblies and constant
wars. We still have many examples of their lovely
vases and cups and platters, their bracelets, earrings,
and mirrors. We can form an excellent idea of their
furniture as well as of their temples and theaters.

While the Greeks prized beautiful things as no other
people before them, so far as we know, manual labor
was viewed with contempt by the leisure class. This
could not be otherwise at a time when almost all industrial operations were carried on by slaves, a class
constantly recruited by captives, and sufficiently
large to manufacture all the necessary commodities.
Aristotle, in a famous chapter of his *Politics*, declares slavery to be in accordance with nature, since
there is always a considerable class of persons fit
for nothing else; although he admits that many
become slaves through ill fortune who ought properly

to be free, and that many others are free who have
all the natural traits of slaves. The higher branches
of science did not aim at usefulness, and owed their
dignity to that fact. They could only be carried on
by those who did not use their hands and who devoted themselves to a leisurely, contemplative life.
Seneca repudiates with warmth the idea that the
practical arts were invented by men of exceptional
genius. He declares that, on the contrary, they are
vulgar devices of the lowest of humanity, and should
be left to slaves. Moreover, Aristotle, in his *Metaphysics*, speaks as if all possible practical inventions
had long ago been made. So the philosophers and
the institution of slavery combined in ancient Greece
to discredit industry. Thus it came about that the
use of one's hands and head in the making of useful
articles was condemned as degrading; and the more
completely one could free himself from such useful
employment, the more prospect he had of rising to
the full dignity of a man and a philosopher.

The Romans took over the Greek industries that
suited their purposes, and these were transmitted to
medieval Europe, with such modifications as change
of taste and alterations in the general habits of life
called for. The growth of the towns in the twelfth
century was accompanied by interesting developments
of craft guilds, and the master workmen in the various
trades began to play a far more important and dignified rôle in public affairs than ever before. More-

over, the common artisan ceased to be a slave, or
even a serf, so that one of the gravest disadvantages
attaching to manual labor in Greece and Rome disappeared in western Europe five or six centuries ago.
The beginning of this rehabilitation of industry is,
perhaps, reflected in the prevalence of surnames
derived from homely occupations. The time came
when no one was ashamed to be called Taylor, Turner,
Weaver, Smith, Fuller, Cooper, Brewster, Hooper,
Chandler, Fletcher, Potter, Horner, or Currier.

From the thirteenth century on, there began to be
premonitions that industry might sometime be revolutionized by new discoveries. A method of melting
iron was discovered, for instance, so that it could be
cast, instead of forged, after merely softening, as previously. The alchemist, in his search for an elixir
which would turn copper into gold, and lead into
silver, and prolong life indefinitely, came upon hitherto
unsuspected properties in the substances he experi-
mented with, and so laid the foundations for what
was to become applied chemistry. Yet no very striking changes in industry occurred before the eighteenth
century. In the days of Louis XIV, when inventors
were already becoming rather common, the people
of western Europe still continued to spin and weave
with very simple devices. Merchandise was still
carried about on slow carts, and letters were as long
in getting from London to Rome as in the time of
Constantine.

But two great truths were gradually dawning on the more thoughtful. One was the importance of the seemingly homely, common, and inconspicuous things about them; the other was the possibility of making use of our knowledge of common things to promote the general welfare. Neither the ancient nor the medieval thinkers had paid much attention to the material world. They withdrew themselves from nature, and, as Lord Bacon said, they "tumbled up and down in their own reason and conceits," and sought the truth in their own little heads and not in the great common world about them. When men of first-rate ability turned from a consideration of the good, the true, and the beautiful, and of the precise relation of the three members of the Trinity to one another, and began to wonder what makes milk sour quicker in hot weather than in cool, and why an object seen through a glass bottle is magnified, they had already made the transitions from the old to the new attitude of mind.

Patient observation, experimentation, and calculation, in the spirit of modern research, did not begin to be carried on in Europe, on a large scale, before the opening of the seventeenth century; and since that time the progress in accumulating knowledge and applying it to the relief of man's estate has been absolutely without precedent in the history of the globe. The story of modern invention and of its revolutionary effects on our life and our ideals of progress cannot be even sketched out here. But it is infinitely more absorbing and vital than the record of kings, conquests, and treaties, and of the deliberations and decrees of public assemblies, which have so long been regarded as constituting orthodox history.

Moreover, what child could fail to follow eagerly, if the matter were but clearly put to him, the marvelous doings of the steam engine, which has shown itself far more potent to alter man's ways than all the edicts of all the kings and parliaments that have ever existed. In 1704, an Englishman, Newcomen, devised an awkward form of steam engine, which would work a pump — a lumbering, slow, inefficient, unpromising contrivance, which was destined, nevertheless, to grow into the most rapidly revolutionizing force in the history of the world. The pump enabled the miners to keep under control the water that would otherwise have impeded them in extracting both coal and iron. By the use of the iron, new machines could be made, and with the coal, they could be run. So, with iron and coal and steam both old and new kinds of products could be turned out in unprecedented quantities; and with iron, coal, and steam they could be dispatched to all parts of the earth. Factories equipped with the new machinery grew up, and cities centered around the factories. So it has come about that the tool has again come into its own as the agent and symbol of man's progress, and that the past one hundred and fifty years have seen vastly greater changes than the whole five thousand years that elapsed between the reign of King Menes I of Egypt and that of George III of England. Just as the use of a stick and a piece of flint began the intellectual development which slowly raised man above the ape in his habits of life, so a new method of operating his tools — the steam engine — ushered in an expansion of his activities, interests, and social and moral problems, the end of which is not yet.

As we are all keenly and sadly aware, the Industrial Revolution, while greatly adding to our comforts and to the range of our experiences by bringing the whole world together and rendering it in a certain sense accessible to all of us through easy and rapid intercommunication, has left the mass of workers whose lives are passed in factories in almost a worse plight than that of the Greek and Roman slaves. It was evidently too much to expect of our western world that it should effect such an absolutely unprecedented metamorphosis of the material conditions of life, and at the same time guard against all the evils to which the tremendous changes involved might give rise. Long hours of monotonous mechanical work in tending a tireless machine or in repeating some minute operation in the highly efficient but often inhuman division of labor on which our modern industrial system rests, together with insufficient and precarious wages and demoralizing concomitant conditions, form at present the debit side of the balance sheet.

As an offset, promising speedy betterment, we have a growing sense of social justice, a higher appreciation of economic and social expediency, and an enthusiasm for democratic education. The unthinking charity of the Middle Ages has become the organized social work of to-day, which is begotten and fostered by a union of human sympathy and exacting scientific research. If the machine has produced a new form of slavery, it has also produced its antidote. It holds out the possibility of abolishing poverty altogether, in the sense of suffering from hunger, cold, and nakedness. For there is now energy enough at man's disposal, in steam and electricity, to supply him with the necessities of life in such abundance that, if properly distributed, no one need be in physical want. What is still more fundamental, with the Industrial Revolution has come a respect, not to say veneration, for labor, which Aristotle would hardly have comprehended. Instead of dreaming of a perfect existence, free from all participation in the task of supplying our material needs, Tolstoi and many others see the ideal life in a happy combination of useful manual labor and leisure. The effect on body, mind, and temper of productive manual work, carried on intelligently, under suitable conditions, and for periods adjusted to the strength of the worker and to his other duties in life, would unquestionably be most salutary. And while we have not yet arrived at this happy adjustment, except in rare cases, we at least no longer scorn manual labor as such, nor do we deem it inherently degrading.

Let us return now to the question of the relation of all this to industrial education, which is in itself but the latest product of the long historic process which we have been tracing. To me it seems obvious that just the sort of facts that we have been reviewing are precisely those which we should be particularly anxious that the boys and girls in the industrial school should be aware of and should lay to heart, in order to gain that attitude of mind which not only would make them the best kind of artisans, but would give them an intelligent appreciation of their work and enable them to coöperate in the process of eliminating the evils from which they suffer. And how can these facts be so easily, so permanently, and so naturally impressed on the pupil's mind as by the kind of historical study which has been outlined in this brief summary of the long story of manual labor? Such study will not only meet the special needs of those whose education we are discussing, but it will furnish at the same time the best, perhaps the only, means of cultivating that breadth of view, moral and intellectual perspective, and enthusiasm for progress which must always come with a perception of the relation of the present to the past.

"THE FALL OF ROME"

I

A HISTORICAL writer is always puzzled as to where to begin and end his story. For his own convenience and that of the reader he is accustomed to divide the past into epochs or periods. Having selected a *terminus a quo* and a *terminus ad quem*, as the Scholastics were wont to say, he proceeds to justify his boundaries as best he may. He knows well enough, particularly if he be a modern historian, that his divisions are highly artificial; he generally confesses this, but then does the best he can to obscure the fact in his endeavors to defend the divisions he adopts. This, indeed, is the regular procedure of the historian, who has to reconcile the inexorable continuity of man's experiences with the demands of clear literary presentation, and, unhappily, he is usually all too skillful in concealing the violence he does to historic truth. The older historians may be forgiven on the ground that our conception of the continuity of history is essentially a modern one — a product of the nineteenth century. Formerly it was believed that heroic men, decisive conflicts, or the intervention of God himself broke here and there somewhat sharply the trend of human affairs. This view could be maintained only so long as merely the conspicuous events of the past attracted the attention of the historian. So soon, however, as he began to concern himself with a wide range of human interests, with the relatively permanent rather than with the episodic and transient, he perceived that general changes are necessarily slow — very slow.

This, as has been pointed out in a former essay, is due to two circumstances. The first is the intricacy of all the higher civilizations. If we consider the whole range of man's interests in the fifth or the tenth or the eighteenth century, we see that no single man or battle or treaty could possibly alter at once the prevailing religious, intellectual, artistic, scientific, linguistic, industrial, mercantile, legal, military, and political ideas and habits. A battle or treaty may change a people's ruler, a great pestilence may affect their economic situation, but there is no instance of any single circumstance producing an abrupt change in more than a small portion of human habits, customs, and institutions.

The second fundamental element in the continuity of history is inertia and lack of imagination. These two mental characteristics explain why even where there has been an abrupt change in a single field of interest a great part of the old has still been carried over into the new. A well-known example of this is the perpetuation after the French Revolution of many

of those governmental peculiarities which were characteristic of France in the eighteenth century.

In view of these facts we can but look with the
utmost suspicion on all the traditional "periods"
which are generally accepted in historical literature;
because they appealed to our predecessors there is
not the least reason for supposing that they can be
defended now.

Most of us were doubtless reared upon the idea that
after the Fall of Rome the Middle Ages set in, and
that then, after a long period of darkness, humanity
was awakened from its winter sleep by the recovery
of the long-lost writings of the Greeks and Romans.
This escape from the Middle Ages, which is known as
the Renaissance, prepared the way — such, at least, is
the popular view of Protestants — for a great spiritual
awakening which unmistakably ushered in modern
times. The next crisis to attract general attention is
the French Revolution. Our textbooks and our college courses still adjust themselves to this series of
epochs.

Of course, every serious-minded historical student
sees clearly the deficiencies of these divisions; he
knows very well the difficulties of establishing the
points at which the Middle Ages began and left off.
It is especially difficult to tell where to place the beginning of modern times; and as for the " Revolution,"
we still seem to be in the midst of that. Historians
do not, however, always perceive the positively mis-

chievous results of classifying our notions of the past under these headings. The "periods" spoken of above are not merely subject to criticism, they perpetuate a wholly wrong perspective of the past.

It is becoming clear to the modern historical student that in the whole history of western Europe there is perhaps no sharper break than that which separates the earlier from the later Middle Ages. In the twelfth century there was an awakening of intellectual interest which created the universities, the revival of the Roman law, the codification of the canon law, the systematizing of the patristic theology; then, too, came the growth of urban life, the extension of commerce, the blossoming of Gothic architecture, and the development of literatures of great beauty in the vernacular languages.

By the opening of the thirteenth century the attention of intellectual Europe was becoming centered on the greatest of the ancient philosophers, and his works were once more spread out before the eager eyes of western students. The so-called Renaissance offers nothing comparable to the achievements of the twelfth and thirteenth centuries. It is true that in the fourteenth and fifteenth centuries the Italian towns developed an interesting civilization and a marvelous art different from that which went before. These have perhaps blinded us to the relatively slight contributions of the period to general change. To one who is intent upon establishing the continuity of history the men of letters, the philosophers, and even the artists of the Renaissance, exhibit an extraordinary intellectual conservatism. They transcended relatively few of the ancient superstitions, contributed but little to the knowledge of the world, and readily yielded to the fascination of Neoplatonic mysticism, as is illustrated by Ficino, Pico, and Reuchlin.

As has been said elsewhere,[1] it was quite possible to read the classics without becoming forthwith Hellenic in one's attitude of mind. It may be safely said that as one's acquaintance with the Middle Ages, as well as his appreciation of our own time, increases, the Renaissance seems to grow more and more shadowy as a distinctive period; and yet many writers use the term as if the Renaissance were a bright spirit, hovering over Europe, touching this writer and that painter or architect, and passing by others who were in consequence left in medieval darkness.

To those seeking to fix a date for the beginning of modern times, three events have suggested themselves as plausible points of departure: the fall of Constantinople into the hands of the Turks in 1453, the discovery of America in 1492, and the posting of Luther's theses in 1517. But none of these events appear to possess the importance commonly assigned to them. The assumption that the fall of Constantinople forced Greek scholars to earn an honest livelihood by inculcating the rudiments of their classical

[1] See above, pp. 116 *sqq.*

tongue among those western peoples who availed
themselves of their services, and that in this way the
knowledge of the ancient learning was once more revived, with all its accompanying enlightenment, will
of course not bear careful scrutiny. The revival of
Greek learning had been going on in Italy for fifty
years before the Turks took Constantinople. Aurispa
and Filelfo had brought over large quantities of Greek
manuscripts, and the Italian humanists were already
busy translating them. It is true that certain Greek
scholars settled in the West after the fall of Constantinople, but there is no indication that the trend of
humanism was perceptibly affected by them; so that
the importance of this event, from an intellectual and
literary standpoint, is probably negligible.

As for the discovery of America, it should be remembered that America was not discovered in the
proper sense of the word in 1492; for Columbus died
believing that he had merely reached India by a water
route. Even as late as 1610 Henry Hudson had hopes
of reaching the Pacific by sailing up the Hudson. It
may seem to us now as if the discovery of a new hemisphere must have produced a decisive widening of
outlook, but the significance of the discovery dawned
so slowly on the European mind that the effect was
scarcely perceptible for decades.

It is hardly necessary to consider the old assumption
that Luther's scholastic disputation in regard to the
meaning and implications of *pœnitentia* opened a new

epoch in the world's history. It is true that within fifteen or twenty years a certain number of northern European states had seceded from the Holy Roman Apostolic Church and had definitely rejected the headship of the pope.   While the posting of the theses was not a wholly negligible factor in the situation, it certainly had no direct bearing on affairs in Switzerland, England, or France.

II

Among the historical breaks that have been made familiar to us by our textbooks and standard histories none is more impressive than the "Fall of Rome." Here, if anywhere, one might be excused for expecting the opening of a new era. The German barbarians overwhelm the Empire, and the long line of imperial rulers beginning with Augustus is extinguished in Italy in the fatal year 476. It has been assumed that the dissolution of the Empire in the West was the beginning of a series of vital changes in Europe, — yet this assumption, natural as it is, is to a great extent a mistaken one. The invasions of the Germans doubtless produced in the long run important results, but these came about very gradually. In one sense there was really little novel in the early Middle Ages. Much was lost, but little was found. A great part of those things that we think of as characteristically medieval, — monks and saints and mir-

acles; allegory and symbolism; the seven liberal
arts; the Roman Catholic Church with its privileges
and its peculiar relations to the civil government,—
these were all well developed before Alaric took
Rome in 410. The "Fall of Rome," therefore, is, at
best, a specious division which upon closer examination ceases to have those impressive and decisive
qualities which have so long been ascribed to it.
The elements of continuity are more striking than
the changes. The following somewhat careful reconsideration of what was happening in the fifth
century will serve to illustrate the dangers we run
in taking the traditional historical divisions seriously.

The Roman Empire was still intact when Theodosius the Great died in 395. It was governed by a
vast and elaborate bureaucracy of which we have an
impressive picture in the official list of offices, which
has come down to us, the so-called *Notitia Dignitatum*.
A century later the western portion of the Empire was
in a state of disintegration. We find kings of the
Franks, Alemanni, Burgundians, West Goths, East
Goths, and Vandals, each ruling over a more or less
well-defined portion of the ancient Roman Empire.

It is no longer possible to trace the process of dissolution in detail; indeed, the changes were so complicated, so varied, and so gradual that even if we were
as well informed about the fifth century as we are in
regard to the nineteenth, it would probably be impossible to give a clear account of the revolution, simply

M

because it was inherently irregular and obscure. In spite, however, of our ignorance respecting even the most conspicuous and startling external and public events, and in spite of the essential vagueness of the situation, writers like Gibbon and Hodgkin have ventured to give us very precise and plausible details about many of the men and events. They, and other writers, have also hazarded many explanations for the so-called "fall" of the Empire. A friend of mine recently amused himself by making a collection of the reasons assigned in our historical manuals for the disaster, and found no less than fifty. And all of them are mere guesses. Even those most commonly accepted, such as the declining population of the Empire and the strength and vigor of the Germans, have been alleged by Fustel de Coulanges to be quite baseless.

The aims of this essay are, first, to review very briefly the general character of the sources of information for the fifth century (all of which, such as they are, are readily available in our best American libraries) ; then to illustrate in a general way the external process of the disruption as it appears in the writers of the time. I shall speak especially of the alleged division of the Empire between the sons of Theodosius in 395, of the events preceding the capture of Rome by Alaric in 410, and lastly, of exactly what appears to have taken place upon the supposed "fall of the Western Empire" in the year 476.

III

First, then, as to the sources, by far the most authentic are, of course, the laws and governmental orders which are preserved in the Theodosian Code and its supplements, the so-called *Novellæ,* and in the Justinian Code. No inconsiderable part of these edicts were issued in the fifth century, and they help to illustrate the organization of the Empire and the abuses which had developed in it; they often give the names of officials, and sometimes even mention events. Unfortunately they are drafted in a pompous, oratorical style, and only become intelligible after some little study.

We have no competent contemporaneous writer for the fifth century such as we have in that worthy retired soldier, Ammianus Marcellinus, who fought under the emperor Julian, and whose admirable history closes with the defeat of Valens at Adrianople in 378. Over a century and a half elapsed after Ammianus laid down his pen before Procopius, the next capable writer whose histories have escaped destruction, set to work to describe the campaigns of Justinian against the Goths, Vandals, and Persians. That there were histories written during this interval is clear enough, but only those which dealt especially with the church have come down to us in a complete form. After Ammianus deserts us we have to depend for the next generation upon Zosimus.

He was a government official (Count) in the eastern part of the Empire and appears to have written in the latter — possibly the earlier — half of the fifth century. The closing portion of his work is lost, and the narrative breaks off with the events immediately preceding Alaric's capture of Rome. He was bitterly opposed to the Christians and ascribes the misfortunes of the time to the desertion of the old gods who had so long protected the commonwealth.

Fragments of other, and possibly better, Greek historians have been preserved, especially by Photius, a scholarly prelate of Constantinople who lived in the latter part of the ninth century. He employed the leisure of a very troubled life in writing out brief analyses of the books in his library. In this way, an outline, at least, of some of the lost works has been saved; for example, the history of Olympiodorus, who treated the period immediately following the death of Theodosius the Great, and upon whom Zosimus relied. Another of the medieval excerpt-mongers, the erudite emperor Constantine Porphyrogenitus (died 959), ordered a vast collection to be made of all that was deemed best worth preserving in the works of the older historians. This material was classified in fifty-three books. Of the little that is still extant of this extraordinary undertaking, the two books containing accounts of the chief embassies are important. For instance, we owe to the emperor's enthusiasm for learning the preservation of a fragment from perhaps the best of the fifth-century historians, — the account which Priscus gives of his visit to Attila, the king of the Huns.   We also owe to him an extract from Malchus, a writer of the succeeding century, telling about the embassy which Odovacar sent to Constantinople in 476.

Among the church historians there are several who have been well known all through the Middle Ages and down to the present day.   The most popular was Orosius, a young man who, under the inspiration of Augustine, prepared a general history of the world, with a view of discomfiting the heathen country people, *pagani*.   His object was, he tells us, to ransack the annals of the past for horrors and disasters of every kind, — wars, pestilence, famine, earthquakes, inundations, and noteworthy crimes, — setting them forth in an orderly fashion with a view to demonstrating that the world had been no happier when the pagan gods were revered than it had been since the introduction of Christianity.   The last dozen pages of this *Seven Books of History against the Pagans* relate to the first eighteen years of the fifth century.   He is recalling events which he assumes are known to everybody, and his only object is to show that those prospered who feared the Lord, while those who clung to the old gods met speedy destruction.   It is evident, therefore, that Orosius can easily be taken more seriously than he in any way deserves.   The most reckless and sensational sermon of a professional revivalist of the present day would be as reliable a source of objective truth as he.

Covering the first third of the fifth century we have the Greek ecclesiastical writers, Socrates, Sozomenus, and Theodoret. All of these are specially interested in heresies, monks, and miracles, and give far less information than might be hoped for in regard to the trend of events. Indeed, very little can be had from them respecting the political history of the time.

In the *annalists* we occasionally find brief accounts of events, although the compilers of annals were chiefly interested in giving a correct list of the successive consuls, and often skip a number of years without inserting a single occurrence. Some hints may, however, be derived from Prosper, who lived in the fifth century, and brought his annals down to 454; from Count Marcellinus, who probably wrote under Justinian; and from the vestiges of a supposed Italian chronicle, which have been carefully collected by Mommsen. It would, however, be hard to exaggerate the vagueness and scrappiness of this class of sources.

The lives of the saints occasionally refer to contemporaneous events, although not very commonly. Some light may be derived from the life of Bishop Epiphanius of Pavia, written by his successor, Ennodius, about the year 505, in which there are allusions to Ricimer, Orestes, Odovacar, and to the troubles of the times. The scantiness of material leads the historical student to make the most of every hint; even the poets have to be utilized, especially the panegyrists. At the opening of the century there was Claudian, an ardent admirer of Stilicho, who sung his praises in very good hexameters. Claudian was, however, not only a warm partisan, but any anxiety that he may have had to tell the truth must have been discouraged by the exigencies of an exacting prosody. The assertion that Alaric was given an office by the Roman government after his return from devastating Greece is derived from a vague allusion to the matter in two of Claudian's lines.

In the second half of the fifth century we have another well-known writer, Apollinaris Sidonius. He lauds several emperors in turn, the first being his father-in-law, Avitus. His allusions are not more clear or reliable than Claudian's; indeed, they are not so simple and direct. We have, however, a considerable body of letters from the pen of Sidonius, which indicate plainly enough that one might live in France in the latter part of the fifth century, with Burgundians, Gauls, and Franks all about, and still carry on one's literary pursuits and escape the summer heats in a delightful and perfectly appointed villa. Besides the letters of Sidonius we have those of a few other important men of the time, of Leo the Great, for instance, and of Ennodius, mentioned above.[1]

[1] The sources for this period have been brought together and translated into English by Prof. C. H. Hayes, *An Introduction to the Sources relating to the Germanic Invasions* (1909).

IV

Let us turn now to the disruption of the Empire. It is commonly asserted that the State was divided into two distinct parts upon the death of Theodosius (in 395), who left an Eastern Empire to his elder son Arcadius, and a Western Empire to Honorius. This notion is so inveterate and so commonly repeated with more or less elaboration in our manuals that it scarcely needs to be illustrated. I take the following statements from two much-used textbooks, not because they are more wrong than the others, but because they present conveniently and clearly what seems to be an erroneous conception of the facts.

On the death of Theodosius the Empire was again divided between his two sons, Arcadius and Honorius. This marks the final separation in fact of the East from the West; after this it is proper to speak of *two* Roman Empires. The eastern lasted for over a thousand years; the western began to crumble almost at once and had disappeared as an empire within a century.

Under the caption "Final Division of the Empire," in decisive, heavy-faced type, another writer says : —

The Roman world was united for the last time under Theodosius the Great; from A.D. 392 to 395 he ruled as sole emperor. Just before his death Theodosius divided the Empire between his two sons, Arcadius and Honorius, assigning the former, who was eighteen years of age, the government of the East, and giving the latter, a mere child of eleven, the sovereignty of the West. This was the final partition of the Roman Empire, — the issue of that growing tendency which we have observed in its immoderately extended dominions to break apart. The separate history of the East and West now begins.

Three, at least, of the chief assertions made above are wholly erroneous. The Roman Empire was not divided but remained one; Theodosius had never been sole emperor; and in no sense does the separate history of the East and West begin with the death of Theodosius. A contemporary would have seen nothing epoch-making in the fact that Arcadius and Honorius succeeded their father, for Arcadius had been emperor as one of his father's colleagues for eleven years and Honorius for three. In the codes a number of laws are preserved, duly issued in the names of both father and sons. The fullest account, perhaps, that we have of this alleged division is in Orosius, who says quite simply, "In the year of the City 1149 Emperor Arcadius, whose son Theodosius [II] now rules the East, and Emperor Honorius, his brother, upon whom the Commonwealth still rests, began to exercise their common control over the realm, only with separate capitals" (*Commune imperium diuersis tantum sedibus tenere coeperunt*, Bk. VII, 36). Zosimus is still more concise: "The Emperor Theodosius, having consigned Italy, Spain, Celtica, and Lybia to his son Honorius, died of a disease upon his journey towards Constantinople."

Orosius describes the conditions with perfect accuracy as they are illustrated by the habits of the period and by the laws in the Theodosian and Justinian codes. From the time of Marcus Aurelius, who chose Verus as his colleague in the year 161, down to Diocletian, the laws of the Empire were not uncommonly issued in the name of two or more emperors. The plurality of emperors became the general rule after Diocletian, and most of the edicts are issued in the name of two, three, or even four *Augusti*.

The existence at the same time of two or more persons who enjoyed the supreme prerogatives of Roman emperor seems to us nowadays a contradiction in terms. It did not seem so to the Romans, who had been accustomed, under their consuls and tribunes, from a very early time to the spectacle of two or more officials possessing exactly the same high prerogatives throughout the whole territory of the State, with only such informal division of responsibility as might be agreed upon between them. The relations between two or more emperors, all of whom were supreme, was determined in the same informal fashion: a son would naturally be subordinate to his father; the younger and less distinguished colleague to the older and better known one.

The whole situation becomes quite clear when we refer to the accounts which Ammianus Marcellinus has given us of imperial elections in his day. Julian, it should be remembered, had been killed near Babylon in 363; his successor, Jovian, died almost immediately after his election.

The fatal course of events having culminated thus mournfully in the death of two emperors within such a brief interval, the army, having paid the last honors to the dead body of Jovian, which was sent to Constantinople to be interred among the other emperors, advanced toward Nicæa, where the chief civil and military authorities devoted themselves to an anxious consideration of the serious situation, and, as some of them harbored vain hopes, it was deemed necessary to seek for a ruler of dignity and proved wisdom.

It was first rumored that a few persons were whispering the name of Equitius, who was at that time tribune of the first division of the Scutarii, but he was disapproved by the more influential leaders as being too rough and boorish; and their inclination rather tended towards Januarius, a kinsman of Jovian, who was chief commissary of the camp of Illyricum. However, he also was rejected because he was at a distance, and Valentinian, since he was both well qualified and accessible, was elected by unanimous consent of all men and the manifest favor of the Deity. He was a tribune of the second division of the Scutarii, and had been left at Ancyra, it having been arranged that he should follow afterwards. And because no one denied that this choice was for the advantage of the Empire, messengers were sent to beg him to come with all speed; but for ten days the Commonwealth was without a ruler.

Upon Valentinian's arrival he was clothed with the imperial robes and crowned and saluted as Augustus. But as he attempted to speak, the soldiers raised an uproar, urging that a second emperor be immediately elected; to this Valentinian replied : —

I neither doubt nor question that there are many and excellent reasons why in all serious emergencies a colleague should be chosen to share the imperial power; and, as a mere man, I myself do fear the great accumulation of cares which must be mine and the various events which may occur. . . . Fortune will, I trust, aid me while I diligently search for a wise and temperate partner.

On reaching Constantinople, Valentinian, pondering upon the burden of urgent responsibilities which threatened to overwhelm him, decided to delay no longer, and accordingly led his brother Valens into a suburb

where with the consent of all men — and indeed no one dared to object — he declared him emperor; had him clothed in imperial robes and crowned with a diadem, and then brought him back in the same carriage with himself as the legitimate partner of his power, though, in fact, he was more like an obedient servant, as the remainder of my narrative will show.

At this time the trumpet, as it were, gave the signal for war throughout the whole Roman world, and the barbarian tribes on our frontier were moved to make invasions into the territory lying nearest. The Allemani laid waste Gaul and Rhætia; at the same time the Sarmatæ and Quadi ravaged Pannonia; the Picts, Saxons, Scots, and Attacotti brought incessant woes upon the Britons; the Austoriani and other Moorish tribes attacked Africa with more than usual violence; predatory bands of the Goths plundered Thrace.

After the winter had passed away

the two emperors, in perfect harmony, one having been duly raised to power, the other having been, in appearance at least, associated in his honors, having traversed Thrace, arrived at Næssus, where they divided the counts [*i.e.* miltary commanders] between them as if they were going to separate. . . . After this when the two brothers entered Sermium they divided the court [*palatium*] also, and Valentinian as chief proceeded to Milan, while Valens retired to Constantinople.

Later, Valentinian during his campaign in Gaul fell ill, and a certain Rusticus Julianus, a government official, was proposed for future emperor; but others advocated Severus, an infantry captain.

But all these plans were formed to no purpose, for in the meantime the emperor, through the variety of remedies applied, recovered and, realizing that he had been snatched from the jaws of death, proposed to invest his son Gratian, who was now on the point of arriving at manhood, with the ensigns of imperial authority; everything was accordingly prepared and the soldiers made "solid" [*milite firmato*]. Immediately upon the arrival of Gratian, Valentinian, in order that all men might willingly accept the new emperor, advanced into the open space, mounted the tribune, and, surrounded by a brilliant circle of nobles and officers, took the boy by the hand and in a speech introduced their future sovereign to the army.

When, seven years later, Valentinian died,

it was decided, upon careful consideration, that the son of the deceased emperor, — also Valentinian by name, — who was then a boy four years old, should succeed to the imperial power. He was at that time one hundred miles off, living with his mother, Justina, in a small town called Murocinta. This decision was ratified by the unanimous consent of all parties, and Cercales, his uncle, was sent with speed to Murocinta, where he placed the royal child on a litter and so brought him to the capital. On the sixth day after his father's death he was declared lawful emperor and saluted as Augustus, with the usual solemnities. And at the time many persons thought that Gratian would be indignant that any one else had been appointed emperor without his permission; yet afterwards, when all fear and anxiety were allayed, they lived in greater security because he, wise and kind-hearted man as he was, loved his young relative with exceeding affection and reared him with great care.

These passages [1] illustrate very clearly the informal methods of electing and multiplying emperors. There was, it will be noted, no attempt to divide the realm among them; if there were several emperors, all were supposed to busy themselves with the common welfare of the whole Empire.

The conditions under which Theodosius and his two sons ruled were precisely similar. No one thought of disrupting the Empire; there was but one Common-wealth (*res publica*), although there had been two capitals since the founding of New Rome by Con-stantine. There were two senates, two completely organized imperial courts, but the Empire, whatever might be the number of rulers, was a *single* state. A new emperor, when elected, regularly requested his colleague or colleagues to accept him, and after the time of Theodosius one emperor regularly chose one of the annual consuls and the other one the other; all laws were issued in the name and with the consent of all the *Augusti* who happened to be reigning.

Viewed then from the standpoint of custom, there was nothing exceptional in the arrangement made after the death of Theodosius; the Empire was not

---

[1] They are taken from Bk. XXVI, ch. i, 3-5, ch. ii, 8, ch. iv, 3-5, ch. v, 1, 4; Bk. XXVII, ch. vi, 1-5; Bk. XXX, ch. x, 4-6.

divided except for administrative purposes, and there
was little, if anything, that was novel in that. No
"Western Empire" was created, and consequently
there was no "Western Empire" to fall in 476.

V

On the death of Theodosius we find three military
politicians of German, or semi-German, extraction in
charge of the forces of the Empire, — Stilicho, the
Vandal, Gainas, a Goth, and Alaric, also a Goth, who
had been assisting Theodosius in his last campaign.
The only way to understand the peculiar position of
these leaders is by noting their conduct in such detail
as it is described to us by Zosimus, who gives us the
fullest account of the years immediately following the
death of Theodosius. We have no reason to suppose that his report of the necessarily dark and uncertain intrigues which were carried on is absolutely
correct; yet the general spirit of the situation is
clear, and he certainly says enough to rectify many
current misapprehensions in regard to the relations
of the barbarians and the Romans.

It must always be remembered that there was no
sharp line of demarcation between the heterogeneous
inhabitants of the Roman Empire and the Germans,
or even the Huns. Probably no questions were asked
about a man's origin so long as he fitted fairly
into the place that he affected to fill. The situation

for several hundred years before the time of Theodosius had been similar to that which now exists
in the United States, especially in the city of New
York. A foreigner, as foreigner, is at no disadvantage
here; there are no artificial obstacles put in his way;
and so, in the time of Theodosius, the Germans drifted
into the Empire in much the same way that the various
foreign nations are drifting into the United States.
They mingled with the Roman citizens in the same manner that aliens mingle to-day with our people, anxious
to be reckoned American citizens as speedily as possible. There was no lining up of Roman against
barbarian; the barbarian gladly fought for the Roman
against his own people and exhibited very few traces
of national feeling. We have little or no information
in regard to intermarriage among the lower ranks of
society, but it is obvious that in the highest rank
there was no prejudice against mixed alliances. To
cite only a few examples: we find Theodosius giving
his favorite niece in marriage to Stilicho, and Stilicho
both his daughters in succession to Honorius. Arcadius married Eudoxia, the fair daughter of the Frank-
ish leader, Bauto, and in due time Theodosius's daughter, Placidia, allied herself with Alaric's brother-in-
law and successor, Athaulf (or Adolphus).

Zosimus tells us that Theodosius the Great, immediately after his accession, began to conciliate the
more important barbarian leaders, whom he treated
with distinguished consideration, and even invited

to his own table. He was known as the friend of the Goths, with whom he lived on happy terms, naming Alaric and Gainas as his commanders and settling a considerable number of the East Goths in the fertile lands of Phrygia. It must be observed, too, that there was absolutely nothing novel in this procedure, which was entirely in accord with the habits of the Empire for centuries. Perhaps the whole situation is best illustrated by the conditions which led to the capture of Rome by Alaric in the year 410.

There had been for some years an active rivalry between the various barbarian commanders, who played the same important rôle in the politics of the time that our alien politicians do in our municipal affairs at the present day. Stilicho, Gainas, and Alaric had each been working for his own advantage. Alaric, almost immediately after the death of Theodosius, had made an incursion into Greece, where he had been weakly opposed by Stilicho; he had returned to the north and received some definite appointment in the Roman army. Just what this appointment was we cannot be sure, since Claudian only speaks vaguely of Alaric's having charge of the armories. Stilicho was very active and ambitious; he defeated Radagaisus and his army of barbarians, but in carrying out his later plans he appears to have encouraged the Vandals and Suevi to cross the Rhine into Gaul. As for Alaric, his first attempt to invade Italy in 402 was repelled by one of Stilicho's barbarian

N

lieutenants, Saulus, but the court party, a few years later (in 408), induced Honorius to execute Stilicho. Zosimus tells us that after the execution of Stilicho many of the barbarians in Rome were killed, whereupon the survivors organized an army of thirty thousand men and invited Alaric to join them.

Alaric was not, however, anxious for war; he wanted some sort of an office, with a due amount of power and comfortable emoluments. He was ready upon very moderate terms to retire with his followers into Pannonia. The emperor Honorius failed, however, to come to terms, showing a culpable indecision, whereupon Alaric summoned his wife's brother, Athaulf, from upper Pannonia, where he had a considerable army of Goths and Huns. He then moved down toward Rome, to which he laid siege. But the city bought itself off with 5000 pounds of gold, 30,000 pounds of silver, 4000 silk robes, 3000 scarlet fleeces, and 3000 pounds of pepper. Alaric once more declared himself ready to enter into an alliance with the emperor and the city of Rome against all their enemies. The barbarians then withdrew from Rome, but as they retired they were joined by almost all the slaves of the city to the number of forty thousand. This is suggestive of the highly miscellaneous character of the persons who composed the alleged "Germanic peoples," within the Roman Empire.

Honorius refused to conclude a definite peace with Alaric, but his judicious prefect of the court, Jovius, resolved to send ambassadors to Alaric to request him to come to Ravenna, and told him they would conclude peace. Alaric, being prevailed upon by letters he received from both the emperor and Jovius, advanced as far as Ariminum, thirty miles from Ravenna. Jovius, who had been a friend and intimate acquaintance of Alaric in Epirus, hastened thence to treat with him. The demands of Alaric were a certain quantity of gold each year, a supply of grain, and permission for him and the barbarians who were with him to inhabit both the Venetias, Noricum, and Dalmatia. Jovius, having written down these demands in the presence of Alaric, sent them to the Emperor with other letters which he privately dispatched to him, advising him to appoint Alaric commander of both the cavalry and infantry, by which means he might be induced to reduce his demands and make peace on moderate terms.

Honorius, however, still refused to ratify the proposed terms. Alaric, irritated by his failure to get a more advantageous position in the Roman service, proposed to march once more on Rome. The news, however, that Honorius had called to his aid ten thousand Huns, led Alaric to repent his haste, and he sent the bishops of the various towns which he had been occupying to expostulate with Honorius,

to say that the barbarians cared for no offices, that they would settle in the Noricums, which were harassed by continual invasions, and that they would accept such annual allowance of grain as the emperor might think fit, and would remit the gold. Moreover, that a friendship or alliance should subsist between himself and the Romans against every one who should rise up against the Empire.

These terms Zosimus declares to have been very reasonable, and he deplores the want of wisdom on the part of Honorius in rejecting them.

The reader, familiar only with the ordinary accounts of the "wanderings of the nations," will naturally be surprised to learn that the Romans had thus early begun to employ the Huns as mercenaries, and will also be surprised at the courteous and deliberate negotiations carried on by Alaric through the clergy. Alaric, of course, had probably lived a great part of his life in the Roman Empire and was no more of a barbarian than hundreds of the Roman military and civil officers of the time. He evidently would have been satisfied could he have occupied a position similar to that which Stilicho had enjoyed under Theodosius.

Insulted by the refusal of Honorius to meet his advances, Alaric once more laid siege to Rome. He cut off its supplies from Africa and demanded that the city join him against the emperor, who had fled to Ravenna.

The whole senate [Zosimus says], having therefore assembled and having deliberated about what course they should follow, complied with all of Alaric's demands. . . . They received his embassy and invited him to their city, and, as he commanded, placed Attalus, the prefect of the city, on an imperial throne in a purple robe and crown. Attalus then appointed Lampadius prefect of palaces, Marcianus prefect of the city, and gave the command to Alaric and a certain Valens, who formerly commanded the Dalmatian legions, distributing the other offices in a proper fashion.

Attalus promised arrogantly to subdue the whole world. This so delighted the Romans that they were "full of joy, having not only acquired new magistrates well acquainted with the management of affairs, but likewise Tertullus, with whose promotion to the consulship they were exceedingly gratified." But the inefficiency of Attalus in maintaining communication with Africa, from whence the supplies for Rome came, led to his speedy deposition by Alaric. He took Attalus to the city of Ariminum, where he then resided, and stripping him of diadem and purple robe, sent them to the emperor Honorius.

It thus appears that Alaric, instead of sweeping down upon the capital of the world at the head of the great Visigothic nation, was pathetically anxious to carry out his purposes in a peaceful fashion. When he found that he could not manage an emperor of his own, he was ready once more to open negotiations with Honorius. The rather full report which Zosimus gives, based very probably upon the contemporaneous Greek writer, Olympiodorus, breaks off at this point, and we do not know exactly what led Alaric finally to lay siege once more to Rome.

The elaborate account in several pages which Gibbon gives of the sack of Rome is largely the product of his reconstructive imagination. From the contemporaries we learn next to nothing. Orosius, then a young man, anxious to prove that Christian influence, instead of precipitating the capture of the city, served to shield many persons from the violence of Alaric's followers, gives one or two instances of the respect shown by the Goths toward the holy edifices, and alleges that the barbarians retired voluntarily on the third day, having burned a few houses. "Recent as is the event," he declares, writing less than ten years after, "no one would suppose now that anything had happened in Rome except for the ruin of a few structures" (*nisi adhuc aliquantis existentibus ex incendio ruinis forte doceatur*).

As the prefect of the city, Rutilius Namatianus, was leaving Rome some five years after Alaric's occupation, he burst into song, and in elegiac verse greets the beautiful queen of the world as she reposed in her glory on the banks of the Tiber. There is no lament over recent havoc, but only a confident prophecy of Rome's eternal and universal empire.

Procopius, a writer of Justinian's time, over a century later, gives in his *Vandalic War* a very contradictory account of how Alaric took the city. Some allege, he tells us, that the Gothic king sent a gift of three hundred handsome youths to the nobility of the city; these young men, when their masters were asleep after dinner, opened the gates to their fellows; but others claim, he adds, that the gates were opened by a matron of the senatorial class, Proba, who, out of pity for the poor of the city, who were reduced to cannibalism, ordered her servants to admit the enemy by night.

Gibbon's plan of extracting "from the improbable story of Procopius the circumstances which had an air of probability" was, of course, hazardous in the extreme. The two accounts which Procopius gives are not only improbable, — they are perfectly contradictory. It may be added that it is to Procopius alone that we owe the oft-repeated anecdote of Honorius and his hen, Roma. While the historic basis of the anecdote is obviously of the slightest, it is one which perhaps merits perpetuation on account of its inherent charm.

Alaric died, as we all know, soon after he left Rome on his way southward to insure communication between Rome and Africa, for Rome was dependent on Africa for its food supply. His successor, Athaulf, married his hostage, the half-sister of Honorius, and carried on, first in Italy and then in Gaul, a series of political intrigues very similar to those of his deceased brother-in-law, Alaric. Attalus was once more set up as emperor and again given up as a failure, so that Orosius speaks humorously of this weak tool of the Gothic kings as "made, unmade, remade, and demade" (*facto, infecto, refecto, defecto*). Orosius also reports a remarkable saying of Athaulf:

At first [Athaulf was wont to say] I ardently desired that the Roman name should be obliterated and that all Roman soil should be converted into an empire of the Goths and be so called ; I longed that "Romania," to use a common expression, should become Gothia, and Athaulf be what Cæsar Augustus was. But

I have been taught by much experience that the unbridled license of the Goths will never admit of their obeying laws, and without laws a state is not a state. I have therefore assumed the safer course of aspiring to the glory of restoring and increasing the Roman name by Gothic vigor; and I hope to be handed down to posterity as the initiator of the Roman restoration, since it is impossible for me to change the form of the Empire.[1]

VI

After we are deserted by Zosimus and Orosius, the information in regard to the fifth century becomes very slight indeed. The annals are meager in the extreme, and the statements of Procopius, written long after, are very unreliable. It is clear, however, that the successive barbarian chieftains continued to negotiate with one another and with the Empire in the same way that they had in the time of Stilicho and Alaric. It is evident, too, that the West Gothic kings maintained the general form of the old government, its administration and laws. We know less about the little Burgundian kingdom; and such accounts as we have of the Vandals in northern Africa were written by orthodox Christians who were particularly occupied with the horrors of the Arian doctrines which the barbarians professed.

In Italy, after Stilicho, the most important military leader for a long period was the "patrician," Ætius. He had had long experience at the Hunnish

---

[1] *Adversum Paganos*, Bk. VII, 43.

court, had been at the head of Hunnish mercenaries, and was well qualified to organize the successful alliance against Attila which led to his defeat in eastern Gaul in 451. He was followed by Ricimer, who enjoyed the title of "patrician" and exercised functions analogous to those of a New York boss.

After the death of the inefficient Valentinian III, in 455, emperors succeeded one another in the West with startling rapidity. Maximus, who is said to have killed Valentinian III, was himself killed within a few months; and in the same year, 455, we have reigning for a brief time Avitus, the candidate of the West Gothic king, Theodoric II. It was necessary, however, to find a more efficient man to oppose the Vandals who were now threatening Rome from Africa, and Boss Ricimer consented to the selection of Majorian as emperor (455–461). He was a well-meaning commander, who had formerly been associated with Ricimer. His chief distinction is perhaps the part he played as "the man with the muck rake," since his arraignment of the official corruption of the times would have been gratefully received and well paid for had there been an *Everybody's Magazine* or *McClure's* to promulgate his exposures. But Ricimer was dissatisfied with him, and in 461 he substituted Severus, who reigned four years, but about whom the records give us no information. After the death of Severus, Ricimer took no steps to fill his place, and two years elapsed before the emperor in the East,

Leo, associated with himself a family connection, Anthemius. We have in Ennodius's *Life of Bishop Epiphanius* a rather lively account of the relations between the new emperor and the barbarian boss. Ennodius declares that Ricimer conducted the commonwealth second only to Anthemius; that Ricimer regarded Anthemius as a slippery fellow, and Anthemius on his part declared Ricimer a hairy barbarian with whom no one could get on. In 472 Ricimer set up an anti-emperor, Olybrius, but both emperors were carried off the same year by disease.

The next year a new candidate for emperor appeared, Glycerius, an enterprising soldier who was supported by the Burgundian king. At the same time Julius Nepos, who was in command in Dalmatia, assumed the imperial title with the sanction of the emperor Zeno at Constantinople. The annals tell us succinctly enough that at Portus, near Rome, Glycerius was made bishop, while Nepos became emperor. On the death of Ricimer a new and experienced barbarian leader, Orestes, who had formerly been Attila's secretary, became "patrician," and he it was who made his little son, Romulus Augustulus, emperor at a time when there were already two emperors in the West, Glycerius and Nepos, while Zeno was repelling a rival in the East.

It has been necessary to review the circumstances which led up to the famous deposition of the little Romulus, in order to see the whole bearing of an

event which has long been viewed as synonymous with
the fall of the "Western Empire." Let us see now
just what information the contemporaries give us in
regard to the events of the year 476. It is hardly
necessary to say that none of our information comes
from any one who claims to have seen anything he
narrates; most of it, indeed, comes from those who were
far removed in time or space from the scene of the
events. Cassiodorus, the famous minister of Theodoric, was not born till some years after 476. In his
Chronicle, written forty years later, he says simply:
"A.D. 475 — This year, after Nepos had fled to Dalmatia, Orestes gave the imperial power to his son
Augustulus." Under 476 he says: "During this con-
sulate Orestes and his brother Paul were killed by
Odovacar, who assumed the title of king but did not
use the purple or royal insignia." It would seem clear
that Cassiodorus did not perceive in the events anything which might properly be regarded as suggesting
the fall of the Empire.

We have the fullest account, perhaps, of the events
in a fragment of an Italian chronicle by some unknown
writer of about the middle of the sixth century.[1] All
we know of him is that, as Mommsen has said, he
was evidently a Christian man of "almost infantile

---

[1] The so-called "Valesian fragment," which owes its name to its
French editors of the seventeenth century, the Valois (Valesii),
may be found at the end of the Teubner edition of Ammianus
Marcellinus.

simplicity," with a style bordering on illiteracy. He writes as follows : —

While Zeno, the Emperor, was reigning at Constantinople the patrician Nepos, coming suddenly to Portus, deprived Glycerius of imperial power. Glycerius was made a bishop and Nepos emperor at Rome. Nepos came presently to Ravenna, but, fearing the patrician Orestes, who was following him with an army, took ship and fled to Salona. There he remained five years, and was assassinated by his own followers.

Soon after his departure Augustulus was made emperor and reigned ten years [!]. Augustulus, who before his reign had been called Romulus by his parents, was made emperor by his father, the patrician Orestes. Odovacar, however, with the people of the Scyrri, coming suddenly on the patrician Orestes, killed him at Piacenza, and afterwards his brother Paul in the pine woods outside Classis [the port of Ravenna]. He took Ravenna, moreover, and deposed Augustulus, but had compassion on his youth and beauty, and spared his life besides paying him a sum of six thousand solidi. He sent him into Campania, where he lived undisturbed with his relatives His father, Orestes, was a Pannonian, who had attached himself to Attila when the latter came into Italy and had been made his secretary, whence he had been advanced until he had reached the dignity of patrician.

Procopius, the famous historian of Justinian, writing about 550, gives a little more detail, but he tells us nothing of his sources, and his data were collected some seventy years after the events. In the opening of his *Gothic War* he says : —

While Zeno was reigning at Byzantium the power in the West was held by the Augustus whom the Romans nicknamed

Augustulus because he succeeded to the Empire in early youth. His father, Orestes, a very prudent man, was regent. Some time previously the Romans had received as allies the Scyrri and Alani and other Gothic [German] tribes, after the defeats they had suffered from Alaric and Attila, of whom I have written in former books. The fame of the Roman soldiers decreased in proportion as that of the barbarians increased; and under the specious name of "alliance" they fell under the tyrannical sway of the intruders. The impudence of the latter grew to such an extent that after many concessions had been willingly made to their needs, they at length wanted to divide the entire arable land of Italy among themselves. Of this they demanded a third part from Orestes, and when he refused them, they straightway slew him. Among these barbarians was a certain imperial guardsman, Odovacar, by name, who then promised them the fulfillment of their desires if they would appoint him to the command. After he had thus usurped the rule he did no other injury to the emperor, but allowed him to live as a private citizen. To the barbarians he handed over the third of all arable land, by which act he assured their devotion to himself; and he held his usurped power ten years.

In the vast collection of extracts prepared at the order of the learned emperor Constantine Porphyrogenitus in the tenth century we have a fragment from the historian Malchus, of Philadelphia in Syria, who prepared a history covering the period from 474 to 480. He wrote in the early part of the sixth century and thus reports an embassy sent by the Roman senate to the emperor in the East, asking that Odovacar be made "patrician," a title which the barbarian bosses had commonly enjoyed during the previous decades. The extract is interesting for many reasons and, as I shall show, furnishes an instance of the carelessness, bordering upon unscrupulousness, which may now and then be noted in the writings of Gibbon and others of equally distinguished scholarship.

The Greek of Malchus, literally translated, reads as follows : —

. . . Odovacar compelled the senate to dispatch an embassy to the emperor Zeno to inform him that they no longer needed an emperor of their own; a common emperor would be sufficient who alone should be supreme ruler of both boundaries [of the empire]; that they had, moreover, chosen Odovacar to guard their interests, since he had an understanding of both political and military affairs. They therefore begged Zeno to honor him with the title of patrician and to commit to him the diocese of the Italians. The men from the Roman senate arrived, bringing this message to Byzantium.

During these days there came also messengers from Nepos, who were to congratulate Zeno on what had taken place [namely, the overthrow of his rival Basiliscus] and ask him at the same time zealously to aid Nepos, who had been suffering in the same way as he, to regain his power, by supplying money and an army and all things necessary to effect his restoration. Those who were to say these things were accordingly dispatched by Nepos.

But Zeno made the following reply to the men from the senate, namely, that of the two emperors they had received from the East, one they had driven out, while Anthemius they had killed. What should be done under the circumstances they must surely perceive. So long as an emperor still lived there was no other policy possible except that they should receive him when he returned.

To the men from the barbarian [*i.e.* Odovacar] he replied that it would be wise for Odovacar to receive the dignity of pa-

trician from the emperor Nepos; but that he himself would send
it, should Nepos not anticipate him; and he praised Odovacar
because he had shown a tendency to preserve the order established by the Romans, and trusted therefore that Odovacar, if
he wished to do the fair thing, would receive the emperor who
had paid him these honors. And sending a royal letter to Odovacar expressing his wishes, he addressed him as patrician.

Nothing whatever is said of Romulus Augustulus,
who has really no claim to be ranked as an emperor,
since he was no more than his father's (Orestes's)
unsuccessful candidate for the office.

We have now reviewed all the immediate sources
of the events of 476. Let us see, then, what Gibbon, in
his thirty-sixth chapter, makes of this extract from
Malchus.

Odoacer had resolved to abolish that useless and expensive
office [of emperor]; and such is the weight of antique prejudice
that it required some boldness and penetration to discover the
extreme facility of the enterprise. The unfortunate Augustulus
was made the instrument of his own disgrace; he signified his
resignation to the senate; and that assembly, in their last act
of obedience to a Roman prince, still affected the spirit of freedom and the forms of the constitution. An epistle was addressed, by their unanimous decree, to the emperor Zeno, the
son-in-law and successor of Leo, who had lately been restored
after a short rebellion to the Byzantine throne. They solemnly
"disclaim the necessity, or even the wish, of continuing any
longer the imperial succession in Italy, since, in their opinion,
the majesty of a sole monarch is sufficient to pervade and protect,
at the same time, both the East and the West." In their own
name, and in the name of the people, they consent that the seat

of universal empire shall be transferred from Rome to Constantinople; and they basely renounce the right of choosing their
master, the only vestige that yet remained of the authority that
had given laws to the world.   The Republic (they repeat that
name without a blush) might safely confide in the civil and military virtues of Odoacer; and they humbly request that the emperor would invest him with the title of patrician and the administration of the *diocese* of Italy.

The deputies of the senate were received at Constantinople
with some marks of displeasure and indignation. . . . But
the prudent Zeno soon deserted the hopeless cause of his abdi-
cated colleague [namely, Nepos].   His vanity was flattered by
the title of sole emperor and by the statues erected to his honor
in the several quarters of Rome; he entertained a friendly
though ambiguous correspondence with the patrician Odoacer;
and he gratefully accepted the imperial ensigns, the sacred ornaments of the throne and the palace, which the barbarian was
not unwilling to remove from the sight of the people. [1]

It will be observed that there is but a slight resemblance between the alleged extract from Malchus,
which Gibbon encloses in quotation marks, and the
literal translation of the Greek.   There is, in the
original, no mention of the word "Republic," and
even if there had been, Gibbon must have known
that the word *respublica*, or its equivalent in Greek,
would have had in those days nothing of the meaning
of "republic" in our sense of the word.   It was simply
a colorless synonym for "state" or "commonwealth."

Most extraordinary of all is the statement that
Zeno "gratefully accepted the imperial ensigns, the

[1] Vol. IV, pp. 50–51 of Bury's edition.

sacred ornaments of the throne and palace, which the barbarian was not unwilling to remove from the sight of the people." Any reader would infer that there was some evidence of the transmission by Odovacar of the imperial insignia to Constantinople. As a matter of fact this oft-repeated story is practically without foundation. In that bit of Italian chronicle already quoted (known as the Valesian fragment), resting upon an entirely different basis from the report of Malchus, we find the statement that after Theodoric had, in the year 493, killed his rival Odovacar he made peace with the emperor Anastasius; that Anastasius "returned all the ornaments of the palace which Odovacar had sent to Constantinople." Whatever these *ornamenta palatii* may have been no one knows, — the bric-a-brac from the parlor mantelpiece, for aught we can say. We are in no way justified in assuming that they were "the imperial insignia," and certainly there is absolutely no evidence that they were sent, as Gibbon and even Hodgkin assume, at the time of the embassy reported by Malchus.

Now, to sum up our review of a momentous century, it becomes clear, as we examine the scanty bits of information that have come down to us, that the commonly accepted notions of the progress of affairs during the break-up of the western portions of the Roman Empire in the fifth century are apparently foundationless. (1) Theodosius the Great was never sole ruler ; (2) he never divided the Empire between his

o

two sons, Arcadius and Honorius; (3) there was never a "Western Empire" — at least before Charlemagne's time; (4) there was little race feeling between the older inhabitants of the Empire and the Germans, who freely intermarried even in the higher ranks of society; (5) Alaric was not the reckless leader of a wild barbarian race which swept down upon the capital of the world, but a prudent and hesitating politician addicted to prolonged negotiations; (6) Rome was not permanently injured by his brief occupation in 410; (7) there was no fall of the Western Empire in 476, since there was no Western Empire to fall, and nothing decisive appears to have happened during that year, for (8) there is no reason to regard Romulus Augustulus as having been properly an emperor at all, or (9) to assume that Odovacar ever sent the imperial insignia to Constantinople.

"THE PRINCIPLES OF 1789"

I

NEARLY a century and a quarter has elapsed since the French National Assembly issued a remarkable manifesto in which it discussed the nature, extent, and general beneficence of the Revolution. After only six or seven months of work the Assembly ventured to claim that under its auspices "an old and corrupt nation had been born again into liberty"; the rights of man, misconceived and insulted for centuries, had been reëstablished for all mankind; privileges without number which had formed the public law of France had been abolished forever. "Is there a single citizen worthy of the name," it exclaims, "who dares to look back, — who would once more rebuild the ruins which surround us in order to contemplate again the former structure?"

Yet not a few have dared to look back with regret, even with yearning, upon that Ancien Régime whose ruins the Assembly so plentifully sowed with the salt of its contempt. Indeed, a writer of our own day, M. Charles d'Héricault, solemnized the one hundredth anniversary of the meeting of the Estates General by rebuilding the ancient edifice with idyllic grace and

195

peopling it with a happy and virtuous throng who had lived together in blessed concord until they suffered themselves to be alienated from God and their king by the satanic obsession of the Revolution. According to M. d'Héricault, the Ancien Régime had served to develop "in the highest degree in each social class those particular qualities required in order that all might work together toward the organization of a perfect society. There was, first of all, the priest, wise, venerable, devoted; then the former despot, now transformed into a courtly and respected king; and the soldier, now a polished nobleman, the soul of honor. The bourgeoisie were rich, dignified, and well educated; lastly the people, pious and gentle, consoled themselves for the lesser troubles of life by amassing wealth, by singing and dancing, while they met their graver misfortunes by the thought of heaven."

But all at once, with stupefying suddenness and inhuman violence, this happy, Christian, monarchical France began cursing both priests and kings; she bowed down before a new goddess with all the devotion which she had formerly lavished upon her old guides whom she would now exterminate — "Cette idole nouvelle, c'est ce qu'on nomma fort justement la Révolution." [1]

It might at first sight seem hardly necessary to reckon seriously with the opinions of a hopelessly reactionary royalist who received his earliest impres-

---

[1] *La France Révolutionnaire*, 1789–1889 (Paris, 1889), p. i.

sions under Charles X. But M. d'Héricault is only one of a group of really important and scholarly writers who, in the interests of reaction, have devoted themselves to picturing the horrors and anarchy of the Reign of Terror. Moreover, the existence of this class of historians can alone explain the attitude of the exalted Republicans, who by no means consent to pass over the utterances of their inveterate enemies in silent contempt.

When the present municipal government of Paris subsidizes historical investigation, it is influenced by something more than scientific interest or even ordinary civic pride. The acts of the Commune during the Revolution have been collected and published with a view of establishing "the immortal glory of Paris" in forwarding "the emancipation of humanity." They show, it is claimed, how the representatives of Paris founded a new order based on liberty and equality, "opposing virtue, patriotism, and self-abnegation to the treason, perfidy, and calumny which the selfishness of the aristocrats never ceased to foment against those noble citizens of whom they might make martyrs, but never renegades." [1] When one calmly considers the rôle of the Paris Commune in the establishing of the first French republic, such sentiments appear quite as absurdly apologetic as M. d'Héricault's picture of the felicity of the Ancien Régime.

[1] *Actes de la Commune de Paris*, edited for the city by Lacroix, I, p. i (1894).

In short, Frenchmen still either love or hate the Revolution as did their forefathers in 1790. A French writer has very recently declared that "the idea of treating the Revolution as an event analogous to other events, without either curses or apologies, has as yet never occurred to any one." [1] This is certainly unfair, but it is far nearer the truth than Aulard's claim that he and his band treat the history of the Revolution in the same spirit in which they might deal with that of Greece or Rome. It will be a long time before Frenchmen will speak of Danton, Anacharsis Cloots, Lafayette, and Desmoulins in the same disengaged spirit in which they might of Cleon, Brasidas, Nicias, and Aristophanes.

Partisan enthusiasm continues to be perpetuated in many important works and must still be reckoned with as it had to be reckoned with a hundred years ago. In this respect the Revolution bears out the observation of Tocqueville that, although political in its nature, it proceeded in the manner of a religious revolution, for it stirred up animosities which in their inveterate bitterness rank with the hateful emotions that have ac-

---

[1] T. Cerfberr, *Essai sur le Mouvement Social et Intellectuel en France depuis 1789* (Paris, 1902), p 113. Aulard sadly comments on Cerfberr's harsh judgment: "C'est étrangement méconnaître tout ce que mes amis et moi, depuis bientôt vingt ans, avons écrit professé, sans éclat et sans talent, je le veux bien, mais en proclamant très haut et en poursuivant sans relâche le dessein d'étudier l'histoire de la Révolution 'sans anathème comme sans apologie.'" — *La Révolution Française*, Vol. XLII, p. 475.

companied religious changes. The explanation of this
perpetual partisanship is to be sought partly in the
French temperament, but chiefly in the fact that
the Revolution did not succeed in settling some of the
most important questions that it raised, notably the
nature of the central government and the relations
between Church and State. Then, the successive
constitutional revolutions, although by no means so
fundamental as commonly supposed, have served to
raise the spirits of each party in turn and so to perpetuate hopes in the breasts of the most radical as
well as the most conservative. Consequently the
first Revolution forms the background of every
debate upon current issues, and the *Principles of
1789* are appealed to with interpretations varying
with the taste, purposes, and convictions of each particular orator who invokes them.

The French Revolution is perhaps the most difficult theme that a historian can select. One who attempts to treat it, encounters every obstacle and pitfall
that besets the path of those that endeavor to make
the present understand the past. There is much doubt
as to where the Revolution began, and as to when it
ceased, if it has yet come to an end. There is a bewildering mass of sources in regard to certain matters,
and few or no sources for others. Every form of
violent partisanship — religious, political, social,
and philosophical — must constantly be considered.
Every one took a hand — kings, foreign and domestic,

courtiers, national assemblies and their innumerable
committees, local revolutionary bodies, communes,
deputies on mission, *emigrés*, priests juring and non-
juring, clubs, orators, newspaper editors, pamphlet-
eers — and to each of these active forces must be
assigned its proper influence on the course of affairs.
Finally, on no occasion in recorded history were so
many changes effected or suggested, in so many fields
of human interest, in so short a time, as in France
during the ten or fifteen years following the convening
of the Estates General in 1789. The most radical
political, social, economic, religious, and educational
reforms were associated with unprecedented popular
excitement and disorder, with foreign and civil war,
national defense, aggression and diplomacy, to such a
degree as to render any coherent treatment of the
whole range of events practically impossible. As
Carlyle said long ago, the words "French Revolution"
may "have as many meanings as there are speakers of
them." To him it meant "the open, violent rebellion
and victory of disimprisoned anarchy against corrupt, worn-out authority; how anarchy breaks prison,
bursts up from the infinite deep, and rages uncontrol-
lable, immeasurable, enveloping a world in phasis
after phasis of fever-frenzy." By Taine the Revolution is likened to the disorders produced in a gentleman "rather weak in constitution but apparently
sound and of peaceful habits, who drinks eagerly of a
new liquor, falls suddenly to the ground, foaming at

the mouth, delirious and convulsed." Neither Carlyle
nor Taine took his imagery so seriously as to miss some
of the deeper significance of the Revolution; but
weaker heads than theirs have been completely bewildered by the loud talk and disorder of the period, which
they have mistaken for the Revolution itself. One of
the most striking achievements of the last quarter of
a century is the relegation of the Reign of Terror to its
proper place. The English-reading public has Professor Morse Stephens in especial to thank for explaining and reducing to its proper proportions the
"disimprisoned anarchy," which indeed seems almost
trivial when compared with the magnificent turmoil
in Russia in recent years.

The merely personal has always been conspicuous
in the histories of the Revolution. Marie Antoinette,
the Princess de Lamballe, Marat, Charlotte Corday,
Desmoulins, Danton, Saint-Just, the poor little
dauphin — these have been dear to the hearts of
readers whose interest was much more readily enlisted
in the storming of the Bastille or the September
massacres than in the origin of France's first constitution and the principles underlying it.

It is high time that we had a general account of
the Revolution regarded simply and solely in its most
fundamental aspects as a *reformation*, social, political,
and economic. This is what Chassin evidently had
in mind when he began his never completed *Genius
of the Revolution*. He dreamed of an *histoire posi-*

tive, in which the personal, anecdotal, transient, and fantastic should give way to the permanent achievements of the time.[1] By the term "Revolution" Chassin understood not the upbubbling of "disimprisoned anarchy," but quite prosaically the way in which the reformers transformed their ideas into acts: how they substituted for a polity based upon privilege, the régime of equality; for despotism, a free state; for divine right, the sovereignty of the people; for favor, justice. Assuredly, as Chassin ventured to think, "cette histoire ne gagnerait-elle pas en certitude ce qu' au premier aspect elle semblerait perdre en intérêt."

But why offer apologies? We long to know just what was actually accomplished. In order to learn, however, what was done and so appreciate properly the place of the Revolution among the great transformations of history, it will be necessary to bring the history of France from 1789 to 1800 into organic relation not only with the Ancien Régime, but with the developments throughout western Europe of the half century immediately preceding the assembling of the Estates General. The older writers tended to give preference, in their study of the Ancien Régime, to the spectacular abuses and the eccentricities of speculation, which may indeed serve to explain the attitude of some of the more fantastic terrorists, but which will never account for the seemingly abrupt and permanent

---

[1] *Le Génie de la Révolution* (1864–1865), introduction. Only the first two volumes, on the *cahiers* of 1789, ever appeared.

betterment. This must remain a mystery to those who have not traced the more or less abortive reforms and the irresistible demands for improvement which lie back of the *Principles of 1789*. The Revolution will some day be recognized as the most decisive and general readjustment to meet new and altered conditions of which we have any record. To tell the story of this rebirth, not only in France but in western Europe, with scrupulous attention to the process of gestation, is an aspiration which, it is to be hoped, will dominate those who deal with this subject in the future.

So few writers have as yet set before themselves quite clearly the problem of discovering and explaining the really great and permanent results of the Revolution, that the public may be forgiven for scarcely suspecting that there have been such results. One exception must certainly be made. M. Aulard undertakes a definite task in his *Political History of the French Revolution* and has chosen what he regards as the two most essential principles of the movement — equality of rights and popular sovereignty — and has devoted his unswerving attention and vast knowledge to narrating the vicissitudes which these two principles underwent from 1789 to 1804. As one reads his book it seems as if one had escaped from wild delirium into a realm of tolerably coherent and intelligible thought and purpose.

Underlying the dramatic episodes of the Revolution, and obscured by them, is a story of fundamental social and political reform which not only serves to explain the history of France during the nineteenth century, but casts much light as well upon the progress of liberal institutions in Europe at large. If we imagine some sober-minded student of the future looking back five hundred years hence upon the French Revolution, it may well be that to him its romantic episodes will so far have sunk into the background that its real contributions to European institutions will be apparent. Among the achievements to which our remote observer will assign an important place will be what are known in France as "the Principles of 1789."

Ever since Burke denounced the first French National Assembly and the "clumsy subtility of their political metaphysics," which, like Æolus's winds, threatened to "sweep the earth with their hurricane," there has been a marked tendency upon the part of English and German historians to condemn the Declaration of the Rights of Man as an instance of Gallic light-headedness. Sybel thinks that the terrible crisis which confronted France in the following years may clearly be seen in its provisions, and almost all writers agree that much valuable time that should have been devoted to urgent concrete reforms was wasted in empty scholastic disputation. Frenchmen have in some cases condemned the Declaration from the standpoint of political expediency as harshly as foreign critics. On the other hand, the Declaration not only aroused general enthusiasm when first published, but appeared over and over again, in a modified form, in succeeding French constitutions down to 1848, and has been the model for similar declarations in many of the constitutions of the other continental states.

In the attempts to explain the origin and discover the archetypes of the Declaration of Rights there have been two main tendencies: the one, to lay the responsibility at the door of Rousseau; the other, to recall precedents in the United States, to which reference is often made, though most vaguely, in the debates of the National Assembly. Sybel believes that our Declaration of Independence suggested the idea to the French. Häusser and Stephens discover a model in a mythical declaration of rights which, they assume, is prefixed to our federal constitution.[1]

The purpose of the present paper is to show how gradually the idea of a constitution developed in France, and how natural it was to preface her first written constitution by a brief statement of the general principles upon which it was founded. It is assuredly high time that we should cease to study the conduct of France's first modern legislative body with the

---

[1] These distinguished historians differ as to the nature of our federal bill of rights. Häusser asserts that it is expressed *in knappen laconischen Worten* (*Gesch. d. Fr. Rev.*, p. 169), while, according to Professor H. Morse Stephens, all the deputies who admired the American constitution said "that no respectable constitution could possibly be drawn up without an elaborate [!] declaration prefixed to it." — *Hist. of the Fr. Rev.*, American edition, I, p. 165.

main aim of finding explanations for the Reign of Terror. Let us endeavor, instead, to see their task as it appeared to the deputies and to their constituents. In order to do this we must review the circumstances under which the National Assembly first announced its intention of drawing up a constitution.

II

Every one knows that early in May of 1789 the ancient feudal assembly of three orders known as the Estates General assembled in Versailles after an interval of a hundred and seventy-five years. In spite of the studiously antiquated dress prescribed for its members, the body was found to have undergone a very significant change since last it met. No royal edict could recreate the spirit of earlier centuries. The inevitable metamorphosis into a modern representative assembly took place during the succeeding weeks, notwithstanding the opposition of the conservative elements.

The intriguing courtiers about the king were quick to realize this dangerous tendency and induced Louis XVI to suspend the sessions of the three orders on the excuse that he proposed to hold a royal session on June 22, and that it was necessary to set the carpenters to work to prepare the hall for this solemn occasion.

On finding the usual place of assembly occupied by the

workmen, the representatives of the third estate gathered in the Tennis Court of Versailles and adopted the following resolution : —

The National Assembly, regarding itself as called upon to establish the constitution of the kingdom, effect a regeneration of the state (*l'ordre public*) and maintain the true principles of monarchy, may not be prevented from continuing its deliberations in whatever place it may be forced to take up its sittings. Maintaining further, that wherever its members are assembled, there is the National Assembly, the assembly decrees that all its members shall immediately take a solemn oath never to separate, and to come together wherever circumstances may dictate, until the constitution of the kingdom shall be established and placed upon a firm foundation.

The importance of this resolution lies in the fact that it was the first distinct and formal assertion of the assembly's mission.

The usual accounts of the French Revolution are apt to give the impression that this famous oath was the unpremeditated outcome of an invasion of carpenters, — of "hammering, sawing, and operative screeching," as Carlyle says; but as a matter of fact the oath of June 20 constituted in reality only a slight, although politically important, advance beyond the state of affairs before the deputies found themselves excluded from their meeting place.

A resolution had been passed three days before (June 17) by which the deputies of the third estate had assumed the title of "National Assembly." The deputies had, moreover, taken an oath upon this same seventeenth of June very like the Tennis Court oath itself: "We swear and pledge ourselves to fulfill with zeal and fidelity the duties which devolve upon us." "This oath," we are told, "taken by six hundred members, surrounded by four thousand spectators (the public having gathered in crowds at this session), excited the greatest emotion, and constituted a most imposing spectacle." Apparently all that was novel in the Tennis Court oath is the clear announcement that the establishment of a constitution is the essential task of the assembly.

The unanimous recognition on the part of the deputies that the true object of the assembly was the drafting of a constitution is quite sufficient to prove that the public mind was ripe for this declaration. By what steps had the French nation attained to a clear conviction that the salvation of the country depended upon the distinct formulation of the principles of government — a conviction which received its first official announcement in the Tennis Court oath?

The motives advanced by the king and his ministers for convoking the Estates General had been but vaguely conceived, and therefore but vaguely indicated, in the Letter of Summons, of January 24, 1789. "We have," the document relates, "need of the counsel of our faithful subjects to aid us in overcoming all the difficulties in which we are involved respecting the state of our finances, and to establish according to our wishes a constant and invariable order in the various parts of the government which affect the happiness of our subjects and the prosperity of our kingdom." The phrase "fixed and constant order in all parts of the administration" occurs three times in this brief document as one of the great objects which the Estates General, in conjunction with the king, are expected to accomplish. The report which Necker, then in charge of the finances, made to the king, a month previous to the actual summoning of the estates, although claiming to reflect the inmost purposes of the monarch, really does little to define the vague terms used in the letter of convocation itself. Necker says nothing of a constitution, but seems to take for granted that the Estates General are to be regularly and periodically convened in the future, and that the worst abuses are to be done away with and the administration improved. No further program was furnished by the government until the king submitted an elaborate and interesting plan of reform in thirty-five articles at the royal session, three days after the Tennis Court oath.

The ideas of reform vaguely advanced by the government had taken a much more definite shape, however, in the minds of the leading spirits in the nation at large, and had developed into the matured conception of a constitution some time before the assembling of the Estates General. A remarkable forecast of the ideas which later became the basis of constitu-

P

tional revolution is to be found in the "protests" of the *parlements* issued from time to time during the eighteenth century. These superior courts of France had formulated the theory of a constitution long before the Revolution, and had, moreover, taken great pains to familiarize the public with the idea.

Considering the inherently close connection between the legislative and the judicial functions of government, it is not strange that a proud and self-conscious body like the *parlement* of Paris should have been inclined to define its duties broadly and extend its influence so as to exercise a certain control over the formation of the law. This tendency was rendered almost inevitable by a custom which had long existed of permitting the courts to protest against, and demand a reconsideration of, kingly edicts when presented to them for registration. This anomalous right of participation in legislation was stoutly defended by the *parlements*, the arguments advanced being based not only upon precedent, but upon justice and expediency as well. The attempts of the king and his ministers to force the courts to register edicts against their will produced serious crises. On these occasions the despotic character of the French monarchy and the problem of the exact nature of the legislative act were brought prominently before the nation.

In order to support their contingent opposition to the wishes of the king, whom they recognized freely enough as the supreme lawgiver, the courts put forward the theory of a constitution. They assume the guardianship of the "fundamental laws" of the monarchy. It devolves upon them, they claim, to maintain the constitution of the kingdom and to see that no fundamental maxims are violated. This constitution was perhaps ill-defined, and was comprised in no accepted written code; nevertheless, the courts very properly pointed out that it was only by continuing to observe certain venerable usages that France could be said to enjoy a regular legal government at all. As they once bluntly told Louis XV: "Adulation itself would not dare to assert that in every case anything that the king wills becomes forthwith a law of the monarchy."[1] The *parlements* appear to have been conscious, however, that their claims rested at best upon a somewhat precarious foundation. They never venture to give a complete or even extended enumeration of the "fundamental laws" of the monarchy. For the vagueness of their pretensions they seek to compensate by solemn reiteration.[2]

Notwithstanding the obvious want of definiteness in the theories of the *parlements*, there is much in the widely circulated protests, beginning with that of May, 1716, which could not but leave a deep impression upon a public that was becoming more and more

[1] Protest of the Parlement of Brittany, July, 1771.

[2] "Le Parlement sent bien la fragilité des droits qu'il réclame et il déguise la faiblesse de ses prétentions sous des affirmations vagues qu'il développe dans un langage solennel." Flammermont, *Remontrances du Parlement de Paris au XVIIIe Siècle*, I, p. xxxi.

conscious of the abuses and dangers of absolutism. The nature of successive conflicts between the superior courts and the king's ministers, important as they were in cultivating a spirit of general discontent, cannot be considered here. We must confine ourselves to the stimulus given by the *parlements* to the growing demands in the eighteenth century for a limitation of the king's powers.

The following statement of the *parlements'* case, made some seventy years before the Tennis Court oath, contains a summary of the claims which are separately developed at greater length in the various manifestoes of those bodies : —

While we recognize, Sire, that you alone are lord and master and the sole lawgiver, and that there are laws which varying times, the needs of your people, the maintenance of order, and the administration of your kingdom may oblige you to change, substituting new ones according to the forms always observed in this state, we nevertheless believe it to be our duty to call to your attention the existence of laws as old as the monarchy, which are permanent and invariable, the guardianship of which was committed to you along with the crown itself. . . . It is by reason of the permanence of such laws that we have you as lord and master. It is this permanence which leads us to hope that the crown, having rested upon your head during a long, just, and glorious reign, will pass to your posterity for all time to come.

In recent times it has been clearly shown how much France owes to the maintenance of these original laws of the state, and how important it is in the service of your Majesty that your *parlement,* which is responsible to you and to the nation for their exact observation, should assiduously guard against any attack upon them.[1]

Even Louis XIV, the *parlement* claims, had regarded that body as "the real guardian of the fundamental laws of the kingdom, and even the most absolute of the kings had accepted the registration by the *parlement* as a necessary condition for the enactment of a law." [2]

The superior tribunals, especially the *parlement* of Paris, are thus placed upon the same footing as the monarch himself. They both exist in virtue of the same fundamental or constitutional laws. Thus, "la constitution la plus essentielle et la plus sacrée de la monarchie,"[3] as conceived by the magistrates, provided not only for a king with "fortunate inabilities,"[4] but for tribunals which had a right to coöperate in legislation.[5] Both owed their existence to the

---

[1] *Itératives Remontrances sur la Refonte des Monnaies*, July 26, 1718. Flammermont's collection, I, pp. 88 ff., especially pp. 94, 95.

[2] *Ibid.*, pp. 95, 96.

[3] *Remontrance* of June 18, 1763, p. 16.

[4] "Bienheureuse impuissance," a constantly recurring quotation from the *Droits de la Reine sur divers États de la Monarchie de l'Espagne* supposed to have been inspired by Louis XIV.

[5] "Que toute administration dans l'état est fondée sur des Loix, et qu'il n'en est aucune sans un enregistrement libre, précédé de vérifica, tion et d'examen, que cette vérification est nécessaire pour donner à toutes les Loix ce caractère d'authenticité, auquel les peuples reconnoissent l'autorité qui doit les conduire," etc. *Extrait des registres du Parlement*, January 2, 1760, p. 13. See also *Remontrance* of June 18, 1763, *passim*.

same imprescriptible law by which the kings themselves were kings.[1]

The so-called *Grandes Remontrances* of 1753 discuss at length the relation of the will of the sovereign to the law of the land. The subjection of the kingly will to law is clearly set forth, and the theory is supported by a variety of somewhat startling quotations culled from the political literature of Louis XIV's reign.[2] This remonstrance of 1753, dealing with the refusal of the sacraments, closes the long struggle growing out of the bull *Unigenitus*. The succeeding conflicts between *parlements* and ministry turn on other matters. The popularity-loving magistrates, susceptible to the spirit of the times, learn to

---

[1] The Parlement asserts, in a protest of June 18, 1763: "Que de même que le souverain est l'auteur et le protecteur des Loix, de même les Loix sont la base et les garants de l'autorité du Souverain; et que toute atteinte portée aux Loix retombe plus ou moins directement sur le Souverain lui-même. Que méconnoître l'existence ou la force irréfragable des Loix immuables par leur nature, constitutives de l'économie de l'état, ce seroit ébranler la solidité du Trône même. Que suivant les expressions du Premier Président de son Parlement, parlant à l'un des augustes Prédécesseurs dudit Seigneur Roi, 'les Loix de l'état et du Royaume ne peuvent êtres violées sans révoquer en dout la Puissance même et la Souveraineté dudit Seigneur Roi. Que nous avons deux sortes de loix; les unes sont les Ordonnances des Rois, qui se peuvent changer selon la diversité des temps et des affaires; les autres sont les Ordonnances du Royaume, qui sont inviolables, et par lesquelles ledit Seigneur Roi est monté au Trône royal, et cette Couronne a été conservée par ses prédécesseurs jusqu'à lui.'" This last quotation the court derived from a speech made by Harlai before the king, June 15, 1586.

[2] Flammermont, I, pp. 521 ff.

give a democratic or, at least, a popular, tone to their declarations. The terms "nation," "people," and *citoyen* occur more and more frequently in the expostulations with the king. We can easily perceive the growing antagonism of the nation towards an unlimited or ill-defined royal power. The clearest and most mature statement of the theory of a constitution which I have found occurs in an obscure remonstrance addressed to the king by the *parlement* of Brittany, dated July, 1771 : —

There is an essential difference between the transitory regulations which vary with the times, and the fundamental laws upon which the constitution of the monarchy rests. In respect to the former [that is, the transitory regulations], it is the duty of the courts to influence and enlighten the ruling power, although their opinions must, in the last instance, yield to the decisions of your wisdom, since it appertains to you alone to regulate everything relating to the administration. To administer the state is not, however, to change its constitution. . . . It is, therefore, most indispensable to distinguish and to except the cases where the right of expostulation suffices to enlighten the ruling power in an administration which, in spite of its wide scope, still has its limits, and those cases where the happy inability [of the monarch] to overstep the bounds established by the constitution implies the power necessary legally to oppose what an arbitrary will cannot and may not do.

While this is obviously an *ex parte* argument with a view to justifying the pretensions of the courts, it is a remarkable approximation to the later ideas of a constitution as distinguished from current statutory legislation. Not only was the word "constitution" familiar to the thoughtful Frenchman many years before the Revolution, but the idea which underlies the modern conception of a constitutional government was ready at hand.

That the superior courts represented the nation since the discontinuance of the Estates General was perhaps the basis of the claim which the *parlements* ventured to make upon the sympathy of the public.[1] It was the *parlement* of Paris which, on July 16, 1787, requested that the Estates General be again convoked, *"in view of the fact that the Nation, represented by the Estates General, alone has a right to grant the king the necessary subsidies."* This demand, passed by a strange coalition of radicals and conservatives, who held opposite views of the meaning of their action, was the beginning of the end.

Doubtless our own early state constitutions may have served to clarify the ideas of some of their more thoughtful readers in France. The earliest collection of these, published in 1778, was prepared for French readers. Another edition of two hundred copies, *exacts et corrects*, appears to have been dispatched to France somewhat later, by order of Congress.[2]   Turgot,

---

[1] "Ce peuple avoit autrefois la consolation de présenter ses doléances aux Rois vos prédécesseurs ; mais depuis un siècle et un demi les états n'ont point été convoqués.   Jusqu'à ce jour au moins la réclamation des Cours suppléoit à celle des états, quoiqu'imparfaitement." *Remontrances de la Cour des Aides*, February 18, 1771.

[2] Professor James Shotwell has called my attention to a curious review of this official collection in Freron's *Année Littéraire*, VII, p. 107

Mably, Condorcet, and others published comments upon our institutions. There can, I think, be no doubt that the hazy allusions which we find in the debates of the National Assembly to the Declarations of Rights in America have no reference to our federal constitution,[1] nor, ordinarily, to the Declaration of Independence, but to the elaborate bills of rights which precede some of our early state constitutions, notably those of Massachusetts and Virginia.

The experience of the United States may well have added somewhat to the precision and vigor of an already well-developed movement towards constitutional reform; more weight than this cannot safely be ascribed to American example. It is in the conditions and course of events in France, not in foreign influence, that the true explanation is to be found of the demand for a written guaranty of their rights

(1783). The aim of Congress "a été, sans doute, de satisfaire la juste curiosité de l'Europe, en lui faisant connaître sous quel caractère et avec quels titres les États-Unis vont paraître sur la scène du monde. Nous ne doutons pas que cela ne soit accueilli avec empressement, surtout par la France, qui a si bien aidé l'Amérique à enfanter la République nouvelle. Ce n'est pas que nous adoptons toutes les idées; nous sommes si libres sous des monarques chéris, que dans le temps même où nous félicitons nos amis de jouer d'une liberté qui est plus de leur goût, nous sommes très éloignés de leur porter la moindre envie." While the Declaration of Independence is pronounced the most important document, the constitution of Massachusetts is reviewed at length.

[1] The first ten amendments of our federal constitution, which form a sort of bill of rights, were not proposed in Congress until a month after the final formulation of the Declaration of the Rights of Man.

made by all classes of Frenchmen in 1788–1789. In
the period of excitement accompanying the attempt
of a hampered and incensed ministry to destroy the
old tribunals in May, 1788, the *Parlement* of Paris
ventured to formulate the principles of the constitution in more detail than ever before. Among the
fundamental laws were "the right of the nation
freely to grant subsidies through the Estates General"
and the right of every citizen never to be arrested
except to be sent immediately before competent judges.
These propositions suggest two of the "rights" of
man and the citizen as later sanctioned by the Assembly. With these propositions were associated a
number of others which aimed to establish the constitutional inability of the king and his ministers to
abolish the *parlements*, whose prerogative it was "to
examine in each province the *volontés* of the king and
order the registration of such as were in agreement
with the constitutional laws (*lois constitutives*) of the
particular province, as well as with the fundamental
laws of the state."

This appeal of the *parlement* of Paris to provincial
particularism, although in a certain sense an absurd
anachronism, was for the moment successful. The
ministry had lost every vestige of public sympathy
since Calonne's financial revelations of the year before, and the effort to abolish the local *parlements*
caused a number of serious revolts in the provinces.
That in Dauphiné not only precipitated the assem-

bling of the Estates General, but exercised a most important influence upon their spirit and character.

Now, this crisis of 1788 is an integral part of the movement of the French Revolution. Although upon the surface the opponents of the ministry were merely defending outworn provincial privileges, which a year later were to be done away with forever, the struggle, at bottom, was against absolutism as such. It was plain that not only were there numberless abuses to be remedied, but also that the king's arbitrary powers must be limited at all cost; for had not the ministers just modified the whole organization of the state by abolishing, by royal ordinance, in a most underhand manner, the last remnants of public or semi-public control? The defense of provincial rights came first, but the issue was really national.

III

As was most natural, the determination of the king to summon the Estates General called forth a great number of pamphlets, especially in the latter half of the year 1788. These corresponded in function to the modern newspaper editorial, which very quickly developed from them. While they dealt mainly with the question of the number of representatives and with the method of voting in the assembly, some took up the work which the Estates General had before it. That of Siéyès is well known, and its author occupied an authoritative position in the Assembly from the first. A less known pamphlet, published anonymously, but attributed with good reason to Rabaut St. Étienne, the most radical perhaps of the more influential speakers in the Assembly before June 20, appeared a year before the Tennis Court Oath, and set forth the necessity of establishing a constitution.

> So long as the changing and arbitrary form of your administration continues to exist [the author urges], so long will the ministers to whom your interests are temporarily confided be in a position to overturn the established order, modify or abrogate the laws and regulations made by their predecessors, while all your efforts to correct the abuses and better your situation will be futile and without permanent results. [1]

In determining the principles of a good constitution, while the author speaks of those of Switzerland and of the United States, he evidently recognizes that England, after all, furnishes the most feasible model. The constitution ought, he holds, to provide for two houses of legislation, a separation of the powers of government, ministerial responsibility, security of person and property, and liberty of the press, etc., — a complete program, extracted in a measure no doubt from Montesquieu. So far, however, as I have examined the pamphlets of the times, the one just described seems to be exceptional. As Sorel says : "The French

---

[1] *A la Nation Françoise, sur les Vices de son Gouvernement, sur la Nécessité d'établir une Constitution et sur la Composition des États-Généraux.* Archives Parlementaires, Vol. I, pp. 572–573.

were much more anxious for civil than for political liberty." We find a great deal more discussion of financial oppression and of the existing social and economic abuses than of a proposed political or constitutional reorganization.

The same tendency is apparent in the *cahiers*, the lists of grievances and suggestions for reform, drawn up according to an ancient custom by the nobility and clergy of each electoral district and by the commoners in town and country. These indicate a very general, if not practically universal, desire that the despotic government of the Bourbons should cease. To take an example at random from one of the *cahiers* of the clergy, we find in Article 1, this statement : "The fundamental [*constitutives*] laws of the nation ought not to be based upon doubtful and obscure traditions, but established upon a solid foundation, to wit, justice and the good of the people." Nothing is to be done in the assembly of the Estates General, the *cahier* declares, "until the rights of the nation are solemnly recognized and determined. A charter containing these shall be drawn up, in which they shall be formally and irrevocably inscribed." [1] This is characteristically vague, and, taking the orders throughout, represents the average minimum demand. Every one seemed to feel that the desired civil rights and freedom could only be secured by establishing so much of a constitution as would insure the periodic meetings of

[1] Sénéchaussée de Mans. Archives Parlementaire, III, p. 637.

the Estates General. This regular participation of the nation in the exercise of legislative power would prevent oppression, if the rights of the individual were once defined and solemnly and irrevocably reduced to writing. Such a course was not regarded as implying any radical innovations. In fact, in the case of some of the *cahiers* of the nobility, the desire appears to have been to secure their own special privileges, which they regarded as "fundamental laws." These, if reduced to writing, were, it was argued, not so likely to be questioned in the future as they had been of recent years. Taine's assertion that the nobility in general held, with Montesquieu, that France already had a constitution, is not, however, borne out by the *cahiers*,[1] although there are some instances which give countenance to this view.

The general desire for some security for the maintenance of the fundamental rights of person and property takes a more definite form in certain urban *cahiers;* for example, in that of the *sénéchaussée* of Lyons : —

Since arbitrary power has been the source of all the evils which afflict the State, our first desire is the establishment of a really national constitution, which shall define the rights of all and provide the laws to maintain them. Consequently our representatives shall request the Estates General to decree, and His Majesty to sanction, a strictly constitutional law, the chief aims of which shall be as follows: [a list of fourteen articles are enumerated, concluding with the provision that] since in no

[1] This is pointed out by Champion in his introduction to his edition of Siéyès's pamphlet, p. ix, note.

society can any happiness be hoped for without a good constitution, the Province of the Lyonnais recommends its deputies to discuss no other subject until the French constitution shall be fixed by the Estates General. [1]

We note in the *cahiers* a perfectly natural and unconscious confusion, or rather fusion, of two quite different demands, that for "une règle invariable dans toutes les parties de l'administration et de l'ordre public," [2] and that for "une charte française qui assurera pour jamais les droits du Roi et de la nation." [3] This expression, "rights of the nation," appears frequently, sometimes with the correlative "rights of the king." But national rights rested after all upon an uncertain historical basis. Should not the recurrence of abuses and the insidious encroachments of tyranny be forever precluded by an appeal to the inalienable rights of each and every member of society? If these and "the principles of the social contract" were clearly and solemnly proclaimed, they would, it was hoped, become the basis of the French government. The nobility of Mantes and Meulan went a step further: "political principles should," they claimed, "be as absolute as those of morality"; they asked consequently for a "declaration of rights, that is to say, an act by which the representatives of the nation shall proclaim in its name the rights which belong to all men

[1] Archives Parlementaire, III, pp. 608–609.
[2] Third Estate of Beauvais, Archives Parlementaires, II, p. 279.
[3] Clergy of Caen, Archives Parlementaires, II, p. 486.

in their quality of reasonable, intelligent beings, capable of moral ideas — rights anterior to any social institutions [!].'' [1]

Nowhere is this anxiety for a separate proclamation of man's natural political immunities clearer than in the *cahier* of the third estate of Nemours, which requested the king to draw up a "declaration" so soon as the Estates General should have set forth the natural and social rights of man and the citizen. This declaration was to be registered in all the courts, published several times a year in all the churches, and inserted in all the books destined for the earliest childhood. No one should be admitted to any judicial or administrative office without having repeated the declaration from memory. This *cahier*, moreover, furnishes an elaborate draft of such a bill of rights, as do a number of others, including the *cahier* of Paris *intra muros*.

This last was drawn up later than the rest, not being completed until after May 5, the day upon which the Estates General met. The committee appointed to draft the *cahier* included a number of distinguished men, and the result of their deliberations is the most complete scheme of a constitution which appeared before that drawn up in the National Assembly itself. The first division of the *cahier* is devoted to this subject, and the representatives of Paris "are expressly forbidden to consent to any subsidy or loan until the declaration of the rights of the nation shall have be-

[1] Archives Parlementaires, Vol. III, p. 661.

come a law, and the foundations of a constitution are agreed upon and assured." The draft of the constitution is preceded, like that actually decreed later in the National Assembly, by a declaration of rights, which the *cahier* claims should "constitute a national charter and form the basis of the French government." No other *cahier*, so far as I have observed, except that of Nemours, contains so clear a statement of this characteristic idea that the declaration of rights is an essential element of the constitution. Not only was this suggestion accepted by the National Assembly, which, as is well known, formulated the "Declaration of the Rights of Man and the Citizen" before proceeding to the constitution itself, but the clauses themselves, as they appear in this *cahier* of Paris, are strikingly similar to those finally adopted by the assembly. The importance of the well-ordered constitutional provisions suggested in the *cahier* can best be estimated by their close approach to those of the constitution of 1791. Among them are the following : —

In the French monarchy the legislative power belongs to the nation in conjunction with the king. The executive power belongs to the king alone.

The Estates General shall be periodically convoked every three years, without, however, excluding extraordinary sessions. They shall never adjourn without indicating the day and place of their next session.

Any one convicted of an attempt to prevent the assembling of the Estates General shall be declared a traitor to his country, guilty of the crime of *lèse-nation* [*sic*].

Q

In the intervals between the sessions of the Estates General, only provisional regulations may be issued in execution of that which has been decreed in the preceding Estates General, nor can these regulations be made laws, except in the following Estates General.

Many more examples might be given to illustrate the similarity between this sketch and the plan ultimately adopted. The *cahier* claims that

the constitution which shall be drawn up by the present Estates General, according to the principles which have just been set forth, shall be the property of the nation, and may not be changed or modified except by the constituent power, that is to say, by the nation itself, or by its representatives elected *ad hoc* by the whole body of citizens for the single purpose of supplementing or perfecting this constitution.

The confidence in a declaration of rights is not difficult to explain. The French nation at large had no idea of the tremendous difficulty of completely reorganizing the government upon a new plan. Few, if any, foresaw that the constitution would be, when completed, a very lengthy legal document. The people, while they longed for a fundamental change, did not care much about the intricacies of the governmental system. They wanted, above all, to secure their *civil* liberty; they cared little to participate in the government, but were only anxious to control it so far as to prevent the revival of old abuses. Two or three things were clear to them: The king and his ministers were wasting the public funds and had got the state into serious financial straits; the ministers, too, had but recently tried to abolish arbitrarily an ancient and, on the whole, popular institution, the *parlements*, so as to consolidate their despotism and shake off the last constitutional guaranty; certain governmental practices were open and scandalous violations of the most obvious rights of humanity; and, finally, the general anarchy of the Ancien Régime hampered commerce and industry and brought home the evils of the situation to thousands who had never read a word of Rousseau or seen a single line of the constitution of Massachusetts. The nobles of La Rochelle explained clearly enough the reasons why a distinct statement of the fundamental laws and civil guaranties was demanded by practically the whole nation.

We behold taxes of all kinds arbitrarily depriving the subject of his possessions; privileged monopolies paralyzing activity; *lettres de cachet* fettering liberty, saving the guilty and putting the innocent in chains; commissions suspending the laws and turning the courts of justice upside down; each minister reversing the arrangements of his predecessors.[1]

In view of these declarations M. Champion is correct in his assertion : —

The classical spirit, the taste for abstractions, *a priori* systems, may have had some influence in the drawing up of certain *cahiers;* but the idea of making a constitution did not come from philosophy nor from a noble frenzy; it was called forth by

[1] Archives Parlementaires, Vol. III, p. 472.

the public misfortunes. Had there never been a *Social Contract*, the idea would have been propagated by the force of circumstances. Why impute to mean or evil sentiments a demand which is so well explained by the state of the kingdom, which had become a veritable chaos? [1]

The French, long conscious of the abuses of their system of government, and anxious to insure their liberties by limiting the prerogatives of their monarch, turned their minds naturally and inevitably to a species of written guaranty which should give definiteness to the chief fundamental laws of the state. The very insistence placed upon the declaration of the rights of man showed that the people had in view a charter in the English sense of the word rather than an elaborately wrought out constitution, like that of 1791. "No one denies now," Mirabeau once remarked with characteristic insight,[2] "that the French nation was prepared for the revolution which has just taken place rather through a consciousness of its ills and the faults of its government than by the general advance of knowledge. Every one was conscious of what should be destroyed; no one knew what should be established."

IV

This brief review of the crisis of 1788 and of the public spirit shown in the *cahiers* renders the attitude

[1] *La France d'après les cahiers de 1789*, pp. 39–40.
[2] Twenty-third note to the court in correspondence with Lamarck.

of the National Assembly perfectly intelligible. The Third Estate, on June 17, 1789, proclaimed its mission to be the determination of the principles of national regeneration. On July 9 its committee on the constitution made its first report, and an excellent report it was. The distinction between a constitution — an established system of government — and a declaration of rights was carefully laid down. In order to prepare a good constitution, the report said, "it is necessary to recognize the rights which natural justice grants to every individual, and to recall all those principles which must form the basis of every kind of society." The committee recommended that, in order to keep in view the object of the constitution, it should be preceded by a declaration of the rights of man, but that this should not be issued separately, for fear that its provisions might prove too abstract if unaccompanied by the concrete provisions of the constitution.

Thus a declaration of the rights of man was to be drawn up in answer to a very general demand. Very few, if any, of the deputies deprecated the declaration, and on August 4 it was decided, by a practically unanimous vote, that it should precede the constitution. There is no need to follow here the somewhat depressing discussion in regard to its contents. It reached its final form on August 26, and had occupied the main attention of the Assembly, at different intervals, for perhaps a fortnight altogether. Was this time wasted, or worse than wasted? Did the deputies lose themselves in vague and misleading abstractions and so sacrifice the best interests of the nation to mere theories and prepare the way for far worse calamities than those which they pretended to remedy? Or, on the other hand, were the principles of their declaration upon the whole sound, general rather than abstractly theoretical, dictated by years of national experience, and well fitted to form the program of their great undertaking?

Before attempting to answer these questions, let us read over once more the declaration itself — it is brief and instructive.

The representatives of the French people, organized as a national assembly, believing that the ignorance, neglect, or contempt of the rights of man are the sole causes of public calamities and of the corruption of governments, have determined to set forth in a solemn declaration, the natural, inalienable, and sacred rights of man, in order that this declaration, being constantly before all the members of the social body, shall remind them continually of their rights and duties; in order that the acts of the legislative power, as well as those of the executive power, may be compared at any moment with the ends of all political institutions and may thus be more respected; and, lastly, in order that the grievances of the citizens, based hereafter upon simple and incontestable principles, shall tend to the maintenance of the constitution and redound to the happiness of all. Therefore, the national assembly recognizes and proclaims in the presence and under the auspices of the Supreme Being the following rights of man and of the citizen: —

ARTICLE 1. Men are born and remain free and equal in rights. Social distinctions may only be founded upon the general good.

2. The aim of all political association is the preservation

of the natural and imprescriptible rights of man. These rights are liberty, property, security, and resistance to oppression.

3. The essence [*principe*] of all sovereignty resides essentially in the nation. No body nor individual may exercise any authority which does not proceed directly from the nation.

4. Liberty consists in the freedom to do everything which injures no one else; hence the exercise of the natural rights of each man has no limits except those which assure to the other members of society the enjoyment of the same rights. These limits can only be determined by law.

5. Law can only prohibit such actions as are hurtful to society. Nothing may be prevented which is not forbidden by law, and no one may be forced to do anything not provided for by law.

6. Law is the expression of the general will. Every citizen has a right to participate personally, or through his representative, in its enactment. It must be the same for all, whether it protects or punishes. All citizens, being equal in the eyes of the law, are equally eligible to all dignities and to all public positions and occupations, according to their abilities and without distinction, except that of their virtues and talents.

7. No person shall be accused, arrested, or imprisoned except in the cases and according to the forms prescribed by law. Any one soliciting, transmitting, executing, or causing to be executed any arbitrary order shall be punished. But any citizen summoned or arrested in virtue of the law shall submit without delay, as resistance constitutes an offense.

8. The law shall provide for such punishments only as are strictly and obviously necessary, and no one shall suffer punishment except it be legally inflicted in virtue of a law, passed and promulgated before the commission of the offense.

9. As all persons are held innocent until they shall have been declared guilty, if arrest shall be deemed indispensable, all severity not essential to the securing of the prisoner's person shall be severely repressed by law.

10. No one shall be disquieted on account of his opinions, including his religious views, provided their manifestation does not disturb the public order established by law.

11. The free communication of ideas and opinions is one of the most precious of the rights of man. Every citizen may, accordingly, speak, write, and print with freedom, but shall be responsible for such abuses of this freedom as shall be defined by law.

12. The security of the rights of man and of the citizen requires public military force. These forces are, therefore, established for the good of all and not for the personal advantage of those to whom they shall be intrusted.

13. A common contribution is essential for the maintenance of the public forces and for the cost of administration. This should be equitably distributed among all the citizens in proportion to their means.

14. All citizens have a right to decide, either personally or through their representatives, as to the necessity of the public contribution; to grant this freely; to know to what uses it is put; and to fix the amount, the mode of assessment and of collection, and the duration of the taxes.

15. Society has the right to require of every public agent an account of his administration.

16. A society in which the observance of the law is not assured, nor the separation of powers defined, has no constitution at all.

17. Since property is an inviolable and sacred right, no one shall be deprived thereof except in cases where public necessity, legally determined, shall clearly require it, and then only on condition that the owner shall have been previously and equitably indemnified.

Do not these "principles of 1789" represent the most commonplace assumptions of European govern-

ments to-day? And yet every one of them was neglected by every European government in the eighteenth century, if we except England. M. Seignobos
reminds us that "when a Frenchman turned his attention to political questions in the eighteenth century,
most of the institutions in the midst of which he lived
appeared to him to be *abuses* contrary to reason and
humanity." Now, if we are not prejudiced against
the Declaration of the Rights of Man by careless and
hostile critics and by the suggestions made during
the debates by Siéyès and others, — which certainly
reached a degree of fatuity rarely exceeded in the most
futile of parliamentary discussions, — and if we neglect
one or two oratorical flourishes, do we not find it to be,
after all, simply a dignified and succinct repudiation
of *les abus?* Is it not a concrete and positive, although
general, statement of the practical reforms which the
Assembly was in duty bound to realize? Was there
not back of each article some crying evil of long standing, in view of which the nation might expect a comprehensive constitutional guaranty?

The Declaration is evidently the result of a compro-
mise and reflects the confusion which reigns in the
cahiers. Some wanted to enumerate the rights of man
before he became a social being; others held that rights
could only result from a contract; still others wished
to formulate only such general principles as might be
associated with the practical reform of existing institutions. It seems that this last party of discretion

and sense was practically successful in the long run. They were not so conspicuous in the debates as the doctrinaire groups, but the obvious superiority of the final draft to all previously submitted is a tribute to the good sense of the Assembly, which knew how to repress the vagaries of the more fantastical deputies.[1]

It will be noted that in the text of the constitution of 1791 the Declaration of the Rights of Man is followed, without a break, by the explicit abolition of a number of the most serious vices of the Ancien Régime; and following this is a list of the natural and civil rights guaranteed by the constitution.

To the greatest statesman of the Assembly, Mirabeau, the Declaration was in theory the "exposition of certain general principles, valid for every political society and every form of government." Nevertheless, in preparing a statement of these principles for the existing body politic — "vieux et presque caduc" — it was ab-

---

[1] Some of the most important articles only ratified concessions already made by the king or reforms introduced by the Assembly in the great decree abolishing the feudal system. The king had promised on June 23 that the representatives of the nation should grant the taxes, that a yearly budget should be published, that privileges should exist no longer in the payment of taxes, and had asked the estates to confer with him upon the abolition of the *lettres de cachet* and the maintenance of the liberty of the press. Then, by the decree of August 11, the Assembly had abolished the sale of judicial and municipal offices and declared all citizens eligible to office without distinction of birth. These concessions of the king and this legislation of the Assembly made sufficiently real several important articles in the later declaration.

solutely necessary to subordinate and adapt them to "many local circumstances." The object, Mirabeau declared, was

to recall to the people, not what they had got from books or abstract meditations, but what they themselves had experienced, so that the Declaration of Rights, from which a political body should not deviate, should be such a statement as it would itself naturally make, were it accustomed to express its ideas — not an effort to teach a science.

This is, gentlemen, a most essential distinction. Since liberty has never been the fruit of theory resulting from philosophical deductions, but springs from everyday experience and the simple reasoning which events excite, it follows that we shall be the better understood the nearer we approach to this reasoning. . . . This is the way in which the Americans drew up their declaration of rights. They purposely left theory to one side and stated the political truths which were to be defined, in such a form that they might appeal to the people, to whom alone liberty is important, and who alone can maintain it.[1]

[1] Hist. Parl., II, pp. 269, 270.

THE SPIRIT OF CONSERVATISM IN THE LIGHT OF HISTORY

I

It is a long, long time since human history began, when a species of apes, probably closely allied to the gorilla and chimpanzee of the African forests, found itself able to go on its hind legs without the assistance of its fore limbs, leaving these free to become ever more dexterous arms and hands. This new being, with his good, big brain case, found that his ability to do things with his hands begat a tendency to use his advantages in novel ways. Accidentally casting bits of flint into the fire, he perceived that they would crack into convenient pieces for cutting and scraping, and so he perhaps made his first tools. What manner of creature he was — whether still hairy, and sleeping, mayhap, in trees like his congeners, the apes of to-day — is a matter of conjecture. The veteran French archæologist, de Mortillet, conjectures that the earliest of the chipped stone tools found in the drift along river banks may be assigned to a period extending back two hundred and forty thousand years. Suppose we allow some two hundred and fifty thousand years back of that for the ancestors of

236

paleolithic man, the makers of the so-called "dawn stones" (eoliths), we arrive at the conclusion that man and his upright forerunners have lived on the earth for at least half a million of years.[1] I think that few versed in prehistoric archæology or in biology would feel inclined to reduce this period, although we have no way of determining it with any satisfactory degree of accuracy. Now to judge from the cavern remains, it would appear that no very great progress was made except in the skill with which the flints were chipped, in the variety of their forms, and in the decoration of bone objects, until perhaps ten thousand years ago, when the so-called neolithic or ground stone period, with its pottery, its agriculture, and its rude dwellings, comes clearly into sight. The American aborigines were still in the neolithic age when the first Europeans arrived in the late fifteenth century.

These facts about man's past are still such comparatively recent discoveries that they have not as yet so fundamentally revolutionized our thought as they should and will. Lyell's famous book on *The Antiquity of Man*, which first brought the great age of the human species to the knowledge of intelligent English readers, was published in 1863. It is true that Augus-

[1] De Mortillet, G. et A., *La Préhistoire*, Paris s. d. (1910), pp. 663 sq. Even archæologists who are unconvinced that the so-called "eoliths" indicate human adaptations do not usually question the fact that man had probably used flint and shells long before the "fist hatchet" was elaborated.

tine found it necessary, in order to secure precedence for the Hebrew prophets, to refute the "lying vanity" of certain authors who maintained that the Egyptians had been carrying on their astronomical observations for no less than a hundred thousand years. How was this possible, he scornfully asks, when not six thousand years have elapsed since the creation of the first man?[1] This estimate of the great church father was somewhat reduced by an English prelate, Archbishop Usher, in the time of Cromwell. With laudable precision he assigned to Friday, October 28, 4004 B.C., the creation of all the terrestrial animals and the appearance of Adam, who, wholly inexperienced as he was, was called upon to devise a complete zoölogical nomenclature. Before the close of the day Eve was created to solace his loneliness, and the nuptials, duly performed, constituted the last act of the first working week.[2] Although some thoughtful philosophers and theologians of the early church had expressed doubts as to the literal truth of this account, Archbishop Usher's exactitude found favor in the eyes of Protestants in the seventeenth century, and it was left for Darwin, Lyell, Huxley, and the anthropologists fundamentally to readjust our historical perspective, not half a century since.

[1] *De Civitate Dei*, ed. Dombart (Teubner edition), lib. XVIII, cap. 40: "De Aegyptiorum mendacissima vanitate, quae antiquitati scientiae suae centum milia ascribit annorum."

[2] *Annales veteris Testamenti a prima mundi origine deducti*, London, 1651, p. 1.

In order to understand the light which the discovery
of the vast age of mankind casts on our present position, our relation to the past and our hopes for the
future, let us borrow, with some modifications, an
ingenious device for illustrating modern historical
perspective.[1] Let us imagine the whole history of
mankind crowded into twelve hours, and that we are
living at noon of the long human day. Let us, in the
interest of moderation and convenient reckoning,
assume that man has been upright and engaged in
seeking out inventions for only two hundred and forty
thousand years. Each hour on our clock will then
represent twenty thousand years, each minute three
hundred and thirty-three and a third years. For over
eleven and a half hours nothing was recorded. We
know of no persons or events; we only infer that man
was living on the earth, for we find his stone tools, bits
of his pottery, and some of his pictures of mammoths
and bison. Not until twenty minutes before twelve
do the earliest vestiges of Egyptian and Babylonian
civilization begin to appear. The Greek literature,
philosophy, and science of which we have been accustomed to speak as "ancient," are not seven minutes
old. At one minute before twelve Lord Bacon wrote
his *Advancement of Learning*, to which we shall recur
presently, and not half a minute has elapsed since

[1] One of Haeckel's students, Heinrich Schmidt, seems to have first
hit upon this method of representing "cosmological perspective."
See Lester F. Ward, *Pure Sociology*, 1907, p. 38, note.

man first began to make the steam engine do his work for him. There is, I think, nothing delusive about this reduced scale of things. It is much easier for us to handle and speculate upon than the life-sized picture, which so transcends our experience that we cannot grasp it.

Two reflections are obvious: In the first place, those whom we call the ancients — Thales, Pythagoras, Socrates, Plato, Aristotle, Hipparchus, Lucretius — are really our contemporaries. However remote they may have seemed on Archbishop Usher's plan of the past, they now belong to our own age. We have no reason whatever to suppose that their minds were better or worse than ours, except in point of knowledge, which has been accumulating since their day. In the second place, we are struck by the fact that man's progress was at first shockingly slow, well-nigh imperceptible for tens of thousands of years, but that it tends to increase in rapidity with an ever accelerating tempo. Our forefathers, the drift men, may have satisfied themselves for a hundred thousand years with a single stone implement, the so-called *coup de poing* or fist hatchet, used, as Sir John Lubbock surmises, for as many purposes as a boy's jackknife. In time they learned to make scrapers, borers, arrow-heads, harpoon points, and rude needles of flint and bone. But it was scarcely more than half an hour before twelve by our clock that they can be shown to have invented pottery and become the possessors of herds.

The use of bronze and iron is much more recent, and the men of the bronze age still retained a pious devotion to the venerable stone hatchet, which the priests appear to have continued to use to slay their victims, long after the metals began to be used.

The Greeks were the first of all peoples, so far as we know, to use their minds freely. They unquestionably demonstrated the capacity of our intellects in ethics, metaphysics, logic, and mathematics, but the incalculable importance of the common things round about them escaped them in the main. Aristotle seems to have conceived that all the practical arts had already been discovered. He was willing that the slaves should be left to carry them on, while the philosophers reasoned on the ideals of a contemplative life, — on the good, the true, and the beautiful. Doubtless some advance was suggested in what we should call applied science, especially at Alexandria, but conditions were unpropitious, and mankind had no better ways of meeting his practical needs in Roman times than he had before Aristotle summed up all the achievements of the preceding Greek thinkers. The great Christian fathers, Jerome, Augustine, Ambrose, if they did not think material things absolutely bad, at least had no interest in them.[1] Their gaze was fixed on the relation of the soul to God. This transcended knowledge. Their contemporaries, the Neoplatonists, maintained that the highest truth came through intuition. Reason

[1] Henry Osborn Taylor, *The Mediæval Mind*, 1911, Ch. IV.

R

could reveal at best only unimportant matters. Both Neoplatonists and Christians were far more interested in miracles and various magical and sacramental methods of promoting man's heavenly interests than in a study of God's world. It was with this heritage that the Middle Ages began. A great part of what had been known in the Fathers' time was forgotten. The textbooks handed down a little Greek knowledge, half understood and mixed with incredible errors. The natural world was looked upon as at best a sort of gigantic allegory. The minerals possessed moral and magical virtues, rather than chemical and physical. The alleged habits of the lion recalled the death and resurrection of Christ, and those of the wren illustrated our dependence on the past. With the rediscovery of Aristotle's works, which were prayerfully studied in the universities in the thirteenth century and elaborately explained and interpreted by the great Dominican friars, Albert the Great and Thomas Aquinas, a new barrier was erected to the fruitful study of nature and the application of knowledge to man's material welfare. All of Aristotle's mistakes as well as all of the mistakes of his new interpreters, became sanctified.

Roger Bacon, the first person, so far as we know, to express an unbounded confidence in the possibilities of experimental science, impatiently declared that it would be far better if all the works of Aristotle were destroyed than that the universities should be engaged in attempting to get at the sense of the bad Latin translations upon which they were dependent. Aristotle, he concedes, certainly knew a great deal; but at best he only planted the tree of knowledge, and it had still many branches to put forth. "If we mortals could continue to live for countless centuries, we could never hope to reach full and complete knowledge of all that is to be known." Bacon held that the intelligent man of science should acquaint himself with the simple, homely things that farmers and old women know about. While in many ways the victim of his age, Roger Bacon, a little over six hundred years ago, gave first expression to the promise of man's happiness that lay in a study of plain material things. Experimental science,[1] he prophesied, would enable men to move ships without rowers, carriages might be propelled at an incredible speed without animals to draw them, flying machines could be devised to navigate the air like birds, and bridges might be constructed without supports ingeniously to span rivers.[2]

These tentative and seemingly fantastic suggestions came — to revert to our clock — about two minutes be-

[1] Perhaps the most striking presentation of Bacon's view is to be found in the following words: "Quia licet per tria sciamus, videlicet per auctoritatem, et rationem, et experientiam, tamen auctoritas non sapit nisi detur ejus ratio, nec dat intellectum sed credulitatem; credimus enim auctoritati, sed non propter eam intelligimus. Nec ratio potest scire an sophisma vel demonstratio, nisi conclusionem sciamus experiri per opera." *Compendium studii*, Opera Inedita, ed. Brewer, p. 397.

[2] "Epistola Fratris Rogerii Baconis de secretis operibus artis et naturae," *loc. cit.*, pp. 532 sqq.

fore twelve. A whole minute more was required before the expostulations of Roger Bacon were really heeded. The leaders of Protestantism had no heart in what we call progress. Luther decried reason as a "pretty harlot" who would blind us to the great truths God had revealed in the Bible. Melanchthon ,reëdited with enthusiastic approval an ancient astrology. Calvin declared man innately and unspeakably bad and corrupt, utterly incapable of essentially bettering himself. But Pomponazzi and Giordano Bruno, and then Francis Bacon and Descartes, about one minute before twelve, began to batter down the great edifice which the scholastic doctors had reared from the blocks they had appropriated from Aristotle. They pleaded for reason and denounced the senseless respect for tradition. Descartes, at the close of his immortal treatise on *The Method of Seeking Truth*, says that he is writing in his own native French instead of the Latin of his Jesuit instructors because he hopes to reach those who use their own good wits instead of relying on old books. A little earlier Lord Bacon published his wonderful *Advancement of Learning*, also in his own mother tongue, and at the end of his life his *Novum Organon*, in Latin. In both he deals with what he calls "the kingdom of man." Augustine knew only of a kingdom of God and a kingdom of the devil. Lord Bacon was the first to popularize, in his varied and resourceful English, the promises of experimental science. He says : —

Antiquity deserveth that reverence, that men should take a stand thereupon and discover what is the best way; but when the discovery is well taken, then to make progression. And to speak truly, *Antiquitas saeculi juventus mundi.* These times are the ancient times, when the world is ancient, and not those which we account ancient *ordine retrogrado*, by a computation backward from ourselves. . . .

Another error that hath also some affinity with the former, is the conceit that of former opinions or sects, after variety and examination, the best hath still prevailed and suppressed the rest; so that if a man should begin the labor of a new search, he were but like to light upon something formerly rejected, and by rejection brought into oblivion: as if the multitude, or the wisest for the multitude's sake, were not ready to give passage rather to that which is superficial, than to that which is substantial and profound; for the truth is, that time seemeth to be of the nature of a river or stream, which carrieth down to us that which is light and blown up, and sinketh and drowneth that which is weighty and solid. . . .

Another error hath proceeded from too great a reverence and a kind of adoration of the mind and understanding of man; by means whereof, men have withdrawn themselves too much from the contemplation of nature, and the observations of experience, and have tumbled up and down in their own reason and conceits. Upon these intellectualists, which are notwithstanding commonly taken for the most sublime and divine philosophers, Heraclitus gave a just censure, saying, "Men sought truth in their own little worlds and not in the great and common world;" for they disdain to spell, and so by degrees to read in the volume of God's works. . . .

But the greatest error of all the rest is the mistaking or misplacing of the last or furthest end of knowledge. For men have entered into a desire of learning and knowledge, sometimes upon a natural curiosity and inquisitive appetite; sometimes to entertain their minds with variety and delight; sometimes for ornament and reputation; and sometimes to enable them to victory of wit and contradiction, and most times for lucre and profession; and seldom sincerely to give a true account of their gift of reason, to the benefit and use of men; as if there were sought in knowledge a couch whereupon to rest a searching and restless spirit . . . or a shop for profit and sale; and not a rich storehouse for the glory of the Creator and the relief of man's estate.[1]

Bacon thus undermines reverence for the past by pointing out that it rests on a gross misapprehension. Living before us, the ancients could not be expected to be our peers in knowledge or experience. He would have the universities give up worshiping Aristotle and his commentators, cease "tumbling up and down" in their own metaphysical exaltations, and turn to the study of real things in the world about them. The reason for such study should be, first and foremost, the bright prospect of relieving man's estate. Like Sir Thomas More, Bacon wrote a Utopia, the *New Atlantis*. The central feature of his ideal community was a national academy of sciences, a sort of Carnegie Institution, in which all sorts of experiments were carried on with a view to making discoveries designed to better the people's lot. Bacon has often been reproached with making no real contributions to science.[2] The criticism is probably just, but his rôle

[1] *Advancement of Learning*, Bk. I, Ch. V, sections 1–11, *passim*.
[2] For example by Draper, in his *History of the Intellectual Development of Europe*.

was that of a herald, as he himself recognized.   He was
the trumpeter who announced the dawn of our own
day.

It was in 1605 that the *Advancement of Learning*
was first published.   And we may safely say that it is
scarcely three centuries since the idea of the possibility
of indefinite progress through man's own conscious
efforts first clearly emerged in the minds of a very few
thoughtful persons.   And it is to Francis Bacon that
the glory is due, as we have said, of first populariz-
ing this great idea — the greatest single idea in the
whole history of mankind in the vista of possibilities
which it opens before us.

The idea of conscious progress was not only essentially new; it could only develop in an obviously
dynamic social environment and with the growth of
historic perspective.   The Greek thinkers did not have
it at all in its modern form, so far as we can judge.   It
is true that Herodotus had a lively appreciation of the
general debt of Greek civilization to the Egyptians,
and Plato now and then refers to Egypt, but there is
no clear comprehension of just what we call progress.
Aristotle was keenly aware of the development of
Greek philosophy since the Ionian philosophers, but
there is nothing to indicate that he thought of mankind
as going on indefinitely discovering new truth, and
he had none of Lord Bacon's interest in seeing the
results of natural science applied to the gradual amelioration of the general lot of mankind.   Lucretius,

the Epicurean philosopher of Cicero's time, doubtless reflecting earlier Greek speculations, guessed that there had been a stone age, a bronze age, and an iron age.[1] But his was no philosophy of progress. Men might, it is true, understand the universe so far as to perceive that it was the result of a fortuitous concourse of atoms, limited in kinds and obeying certain fixed laws. But the chief significance of this to Lucretius lay in abolishing all fear of the gods and of death. He did not discover in his mechanistic universe any promise of steady human progress. Indeed, he thought that a degeneration was setting in which foreboded the complete dissolution of the universe as we know it. In short, the Greek and Roman philosophers would have agreed with the medieval theologians in accepting the stationary character of the civilization with which they were familiar.

Augustine and his disciple, Orosius, gave history a new background, and illustrated God's dealings with man, from the Garden of Eden to the sack of Rome by Alaric; but they knew little or nothing of man's long history and unconscious progress in the past, nor did they anticipate any future improvement, for to the ardent Christian no earthly betterment

[1] In the oft-quoted and remarkable lines: —

Arma antiqua manus, ungues, dentesque fuerunt
Et lapides, et item sylvarum fragmina rami,
Posterius ferri vis est aerisque reperta;
Sed prior aeris erat quam ferri cognitus usus.
    — *De rerum natura*, Bk. V, vv. 1281 sqq.

could compare with the overwhelming issue which awaited man after death, when every one entered into eternal and unchanging bliss or misery. Accordingly, emulation consisted at best, until the opening of the seventeenth century, in striving to reach standards set by the past. The mere age of an institution or a belief came to be its surest sanction. The present might consider itself fortunate if it was at any point as good as the past. Only with Giordano Bruno and Lord Bacon did the strength of authority and tradition begin to be weakened, in spite of the hostility and consistent opposition of those who believed that they were defending God-given arrangements against the attacks of infidels, freethinkers, and rationalists.[1]

The process of weakening authority has been very rapid, considering its novelty and its fundamental character. It went on apace in the eighteenth century. Beccaria, the Italian jurist, who pleaded so eloquently for the revision of the horrible criminal law, foresaw that the conservatives would urge that the practices which he sought to abolish were ratified by a hoary past; he begged them to recollect that the past was after all only an immense sea of errors from which there emerged here and there an obscure truth.[2] Dur-

---

[1] This cursory treatment of a great theme, the origin of the idea of progress, may be supplemented by Delvaille, J., *Essai sur l'histoire de l'idée de Progrès jusqu'à la fin du XVIIIième Siècle*, 1910; Laurent, *Études sur l'histoire de l'humanité*, 1866, Ch. XII, pp. 63 sqq.; and Flint, *History of the Philosophy of History*, pp. 88 sqq.

[2] Beccaria, *An Essay on Crimes and Punishments*, 1788, p. 113.

ing the early years of the French Revolution, and under most discouraging circumstances, Condorcet wrote his famous treatise on the indefinite perfectibility of man. In it he seeks to trace the steps which humanity has taken in the past toward truth and happiness. "Ces observations," he trusts, "sur ce que l'homme a été, sur ce qu'il est aujourd'hui, conduiront ensuite aux moyens d'assurer et d'accélérer les nouveaux progrès que sa nature lui permet d'espérer encore. Tel est le but de l'ouvrage que j'ai enterpris, et dont le résultat sera de montrer, par le raisonnement et par les faits, qu'il n'a été marqué aucun terme au perfectionnement des facultés humaines, que la perfectibilité de l'homme est réellement indéfinie; que les progrès de cette perfectibilité, désormais indépendent de toute puissance qui voudrait l'arrêter, n'ont d'autre terme que la durée du globe où la nature nous a jetés."[1]

These genial speculations tending to turn men's eyes toward the future rather than the past were tremendously reënforced by the scientific discoveries of the nineteenth century. These proved, first, that man was learning a great deal more than any one had ever known before about the world and his place in it. Secondly, he was applying his knowledge in such a way as to make older methods of manufacture and transportation and communication appear very crude

[1] "Esquisse d'un tableau historique des progrès de l'esprit humain," 1797, p. 4.

and antiquated. Lastly, Darwin, Lyell, Boucher de Perthes, Huxley, G. de Mortillet, Haeckel, and the rest established the fact that long before historic times man had proved himself capable of the most startling progress. He had not only made his way from savagery to civilization, but from the estate of an animal to that of a man. Not only had his ancestors gone on all fours and lived as the beasts of the field, but their remoter ancestors had mayhap lived in the sea and, as Darwin conjectures, resembled a so-called Ascidian larva, a tadpole-like creature not yet supplied with an unmistakable backbone. Roger Bacon, Francis Bacon, Descartes, Beccaria, Condorcet, — these and many like them stoutly maintained that man could learn indefinitely more than any of his predecessors had known, and could better his estate indefinitely by the use of this knowledge and the desertion of ancient prejudices and habits. The nineteenth century proved conclusively that he *had* been learning and *had* been bettering himself for hundreds of thousands of years. But all this earlier progress had been *unconscious*. For the first time, close upon our own day, progress became an ideal consciously proclaimed and sought. So, whatever the progress of man has been during the twelve hours which we assign to him since he became man, it was only at about one minute to twelve *that he came to wish to progress, and still more recently that he came to see that he can voluntarily progress, and that he has progressed.* This appears to

me to be the most impressive message that history
has to give us, and the most vital in the light that it
casts on the conduct of life.

II

If it be conceded that what we rather vaguely and
provisionally call social betterment is coming to be
regarded by large numbers of thoughtful persons as
the chief interest in this game of life, does not the
supreme value of history lie for us to-day in the suggestions that it may give us of what may be called
the technique of progress, and ought not those phases
of the past especially to engross our attention which
bear on this essential point? History has been regularly invoked, to substantiate the claims of the
conservative, but has hitherto usually been neglected
by the radical,[1] or impatiently repudiated as the
chosen weapon of his enemy. The radical has not yet
perceived the overwhelming value to him of a real
understanding of the past. It is his weapon by right,
and he should wrest it from the hand of the conservative. It has received a far keener edge during the
last century, and it is the chief end of this essay to
indicate how it can be used with the most decisive
effect on the conservative.

So far as I know, no satisfactory analysis has ever

[1] The Marxian socialist, of course, uses his version of the past in
support of his plan of social amelioration.

been made of the conservative and radical temperaments. It is commonly assumed that every boy and girl is born into one or the other party, and doubtless as mere animals we differ greatly in our bravery, energy, and hopefulness. But nurture is now seen to be all that separates even the most uncompromising radical from a life far lower than that of any savage that exists on the earth at the present time. Even the recently extinct race of Tasmanians, still in a paleolithic stage of development, represented achievements which it took man long ages to accumulate. The literally uneducated European even to-day could neither frame a sentence nor sharpen a stick with a shell. A great part, then, of all that goes to make up the conservative or radical may be deemed the result of education in the broadest sense of that term, including everything that he has got from associating since infancy with civilized companions. I think that the modern anthropologist and psychologist would agree on this point; at least, every one who allows his mind to play freely over the question must concede that a great part of what has been mistaken for *nature* is really *nurture*, direct and indirect, conscious or, more commonly, wholly unconscious.

Now it has been the constant objection urged by the conservative against any reform of which he disapproved that it involved a change of human nature. He has flattered himself that he knew the chief characteristics of humanity and that, since it was hopeless to alter any of these, a change which seemed to imply such an alteration was obviously impracticable. This argument was long ago met by Montaigne, who declared that one who viewed Mother Nature in her full majesty and luster might perceive so general and so constant a variety that any individual and even the whole kingdom in which he happened to live must seem but a pin's point in comparison.[1] But there is a wholly new argument now available. Whether the zoölogists are quite right or no in denying the possibility of the hereditary transmission of acquired traits, there is no reason to think that one particle of culture ever gets into the blood of our human species; it must either be transmitted by imitation or inculcation, or be lost, as Gabriel Tarde has made clear. We doubtless inherit the aptitudes of our parents, grandparents, and remoter ancestors; but any actual exercise that they may have made of the faculties which we share with them cannot influence us except by example or emulation. *Those things that the radical would alter and the conservative defend are therefore not traits of human nature but artificial achievements of human nurture.* Accordingly, the anthropologist and historian can rule out this fundamental conservative appeal to human nature by showing that the most extraordinary variety has existed and still exists in the habits, institutions, and feelings of various groups of mankind; and the student familiar with the chief

[1] "On Education," *Essays*, Bk. I, Ch. XXV.

results of embryology will see that the conservative has constantly mistaken the artificially acquired and hereditarily non-transmissible for constant and unalterable elements in our native outfit. And, indeed, it may be asked, if it has proved possible to alter an invertebrate tadpole-like creature living in the sea into an ape-like animal sleeping in a tree, and to transform the ape-like animal into an ingenious flint-chipping artist, able to paint pictures of bison and deer on the walls of a cave, and to derive from the flint chipper of the stone age a Plato able to tell a most edifying tale about a cave full of conservatives, what becomes of the argument for the fixity of human nature in any important sense?

While it is then highly unscientific and unhistorical to consider the way in which men behave and feel at any particular time as exhibiting the normal and immutable principles of human nature, history and anthropology nevertheless concur in proving that each new generation is indebted to the previous generation for very nearly all that it is and has. This is true of even the most rapidly progressing societies, and there is reason to suppose that a group of mankind could live indefinitely adhering to an unchanged scheme of civilization so long as they were undisturbed and their environment remained constant. We have seen how very recently the idea that progress is possible has dawned upon a small portion of mankind. The alterations which any people can effect

within a half century in its prevailing ideas and institutions, and in the range and character of its generally diffused knowledge, are necessarily slight when
compared with the vast heritage which has gradually
been accumulating during hundreds of thousands
of years. In order to make the nature and variety
of our abject dependence on the past clear, we have
only to consider our language, our laws, our political
and social institutions, our knowledge and education,
our view of this world and the next, our tastes and the
means of gratifying them. On every hand the past
dominates and controls us, for the most part unconsciously and without protest on our part. We are
in the main its willing adherents. The imagination
of the most radically-minded cannot transcend any
great part of the ideas and customs transmitted to
him. When once we grasp this truth, we shall, according to our mood, humbly congratulate ourselves that,
poor pygmies that we are, we are permitted to stand
on the giant's shoulders and enjoy an outlook that
would be quite hidden from us if we had to trust to
our own short legs ; or we may resentfully chafe at our
bonds and, like Prometheus, vainly strive to wrest
ourselves from the rock of the past, in our eagerness
to bring relief to the suffering children of men.

> Es erben sich Gesetz' und Rechte
> Wie eine ew'ge Krankheit fort.

In any case, whether we bless or curse the past, we
are inevitably its offspring, and it makes us its own

long before we realize it.   It is, indeed, almost all that
we can have.   The most frantic of us must follow
the beaten path; we are like a squirrel in his revolv-
ing cage.

There is no space here to discuss the general relation of history to the causes and technique of progress,
but a word may be said of the effect which our modern
outlook should have on our estimate of the conservative mood.   Mr. John Morley has given an unpleas-
ant but not inaccurate sketch of the conservative,
"with his inexhaustible patience of abuses that only
torment others; his apologetic word for beliefs that
may not be so precisely true as one might wish, and
institutions that are not altogether so useful as some
might think possible; his cordiality towards progress
and improvement in a general way, and his coldness
or antipathy to each progressive proposal in particular;
his pygmy hope that life will one day become somewhat
better, punily shivering by the side of his gigantic
conviction that it might well be infinitely worse."
How numerous and how respectable is still this class !
It is made up of clergymen, lawyers, teachers, editors,
and successful men of affairs.   Doubtless some of
them are nervous and apologetic, and try to find
reasons to disguise their general opposition to change
by taking credit for improvements to which they contribute nothing, or by forwarding some minor changes
which exhaust their powers of imagination and
innovation.   But how rarely does one of them fail,
s

when he addresses the young, to utter some warning, some praise of the past, some discouragement to effort and the onward struggle! The conservative is a perfectly explicable and inevitable product of that long, long period before man woke up to the possibility of conscious betterment. He still justifies existing conditions and ideas by the standards of the past rather than by those of the present or future. He neither vividly realizes how mightily things have advanced in times gone by, nor has he the imagination to see how easily they could be indefinitely bettered, if the temperament which he represents could cease to be artificially fostered.

Should the conservative be roused to defend himself, having been driven from the protection which his discredited conception of "human nature" formerly offered, he may ask peevishly, "what does progress mean anyway?" But no one who realizes the relative barbarism of our whole civilization, which contains, on a fair appraisal, so little to cheer us except promises for the future, will have the patience to formulate any general definition of progress when the most bewildering opportunities for betterment summon us on every side. What can the conservative point to that is not susceptible of improvement?

There is one more solace, perhaps the last, for the hard-pressed conservative. He may heartily agree that much improvement has taken place and claim that he views with deep satisfaction all deliberate and decorous progress, but ascribe to himself the modest and perhaps ungrateful function of acting as a brake which prevents the chariot of progress from rushing headlong down a decline. But is there any reason to suppose that any brake is necessary? Have fiery radicals ever got possession of the reins and actually driven for a time at a breakneck speed? The conservative would find it extremely difficult to cite historic examples, but doubtless the Reign of Terror would occur to him as an instance. This certainly has more plausibility than any other alleged example in the whole recorded history of mankind. But Camille Desmoulins, one of its most amiable victims, threw the blame of the whole affair, with much sound reasoning, on the precious conservatives themselves. And I think that all scholars would agree that the incapable and traitorous Louis XVI and his runaway nobles, supported by the threats of the monarchs of Prussia and Austria, were at the bottom of the whole matter. In any case, as Desmoulins urges, the blood shed in the cause of liberty was as nothing to that which had been spilt by kings and prelates in maintaining their dominion and satisfying their ambitions.[1]

So even this favorite instance of o'er-rapid change will scarcely bear impartial scrutiny, and we may safely assert that so far the chariot of progress has always been toiling up a steep incline and that the

[1] "Vieux Cordelier," No. 3, December, 1793.

restraining brake of the conservatives has been worse than useless. Maeterlinck exhorts us never to fear that we shall be drawn too far or too rapidly; and there is certainly nothing in the past or present to justify this fear. On the contrary, as he says, "There are men enough about us whose exclusive duty, whose precise mission, is to extinguish the fires that we kindle." "At every crossway on the road that leads to the future, each progressive spirit is opposed by a thousand men appointed to guard the past. Let us have no fear lest the fairest towers of former days be sufficiently defended. The least that the most timid among us can do is not to add to the immense deadweight which nature drags along."

History, the whole history of man and of the organic universe, seems now to put the conservative arguments to shame. Indeed it seems to do more; it seems to justify the mystic confidence in the future suggested in Maeterlinck's *Our Social Duty*. Perhaps, as he believes, an excess of radicalism is essential to the equilibrium of life. "Let us not say to ourselves," he urges, "that the best truth always lies in moderation, in the decent average. This would perhaps be so if the majority of men did not think on a much lower plane than is needful. That is why it behooves others to think and hope on a higher plane than seems reasonable. The average, the decent moderation of to-day, will be the least human of things to-morrow. At the time of the Spanish Inquisition, the opinion of good

sense and of the just medium was certainly that people
ought not to burn too large a number of heretics;
extreme and unreasonable opinion obviously demanded
that they should burn none at all."

Here again we may turn to the past for its authenti-
cating testimony. A society without slaves would
have been almost incomprehensible to Plato and Aristotle. To the latter slavery was an inevitable corollary
of human society. To Innocent III a church without
graft was a hopeless ideal. To Richelieu a foreign
service without bribery was a myth. To Beccaria a
criminal procedure without torture, and courts without
corrupt judges, were a dream. It would have seemed
preposterous enough to Franklin to forecast a time
when a Philadelphian could converse in his home with
friends far beyond the Mississippi, or to assert that
one day letters would be carried to all parts of the earth
for so small a sum that even the poorest would not
find the expense an obstacle to communication. But
all these hopeless, preposterous dreams have come to
pass and that in a little more than a hundred years.

From forwarding these achievements the conservative has hitherto held himself aloof, whether from temperament, ignorance, or despair. But let us exonerate
him, for he knew no better. He had not the wit to
see that he was a vestige of a long, unenlightened
epoch. But history would seem to show that this
period of exemption from service is now at an end. It
is plain that his theory that human nature cannot be

altered is exploded, as well as his belief that a fractious world needs him to apply the brakes.

The conservative has, in short, been victimized by a misunderstood past. Hitherto the radical has appealed to the future, but now he can confidently rest his case on past achievement and current success. He can point to what has been done, he can cite what is being done, he can perceive as never before what remains to be done, and, lastly, he begins to see, as never before, how it will get done. It has been the chief business of this essay to suggest what has been done. If there were time, I might try to show that progress in knowledge and its application to the alleviation of man's estate is more rapid now than ever before. But this scarcely needs formal proof; it is so obvious. A few years ago an eminent French litterateur, Brunetière, declared science bankrupt. This was on the eve of the discoveries in radioactivity which have opened up great vistas of possible human readjustments if we could but learn to control and utilize the inexhaustible sources of power that lie within the atom. It was on the eve of the discovery of the functions of the white blood corpuscles, which clears the way for indefinite advance in medicine. Only a poor discouraged man of letters could think for a moment that science was bankrupt. No one entitled to an opinion on the subject believes that we have made more than a beginning in penetrating the secrets of the organic and inorganic world.

In the fourth canto of the *Inferno* Dante describes the confines of hell. Here he heard sighs which made the eternal air to tremble. These came of the woe felt by multitudes, which were many and great, of infants and of women and men who, although they had lived guiltless lives, were condemned for being born before the true religion had been revealed. They lived without hope. But in the midst of the gloom he beheld a fire that conquered a hemisphere of darkness. Here, in a place open, luminous, and high, people with eyes slow and grave, of great authority in their looks, sat on the greensward, speaking seldom and with soft voices. These were the ancient philosophers, statesmen, military heroes, and men of letters. Neither sad nor glad, they held high discourse, heedless of the wails of infants, unconscious of the horrors of hell which boiled beneath them. They knew nothing of the mountain of purgatorial progress on the other side of the earth, which others were climbing, and heaven was forever inaccessible to them. Yet why should they regret it — were they not already in the only heaven they were fit for?

As for accomplishing the great reforms that demand our united efforts — the abolition of poverty and disease and war, and the promotion of happy and rational lives — the task would seem hopeless enough were it not for the considerations which have been recalled above. Until very recently the leaders of men have looked backward for their standards and ideals. The intellectual ancestors of the conservative extend back in an unbroken line to the very beginning of human history. The reformer who appeals to the future is a recent upstart. He belongs to the last half minute of our historical reckoning. His family is a new one, and its members have often seemed very black sheep to the good old family of conservatives who have found no names too terrible to apply to the Anthony Collinses, the Voltaires and Tom Paines, who now seem so innocent and commonplace in most of their teachings. But it is clear enough to-day that the conscious reformer who appeals to the future is the final product of a progressive order of things. While the conservative sullenly opposed what were in Roger Bacon's time called "suspicious novelties," and condemned changes either as wicked or impracticable, he was himself being gradually drawn along in a process of insensible betterment in which he refused consciously to participate. Even those of us who have little taste for mysticism have to recognize a mysterious unconscious impulse which appears to be a concomitant of natural order. It would seem as if this impulse has always been unsettling the existing conditions and pushing forward, groping after something more elaborate and intricate than what already existed. This vital impulse, *élan vital*, as Bergson calls it, represents the inherent radicalism of nature herself. This power that makes for experimental readjustment, — for *adventure* in the broadest sense of the term, — is no longer a conception confined to poets and dreamers, but must be reckoned with by the most exacting historian and the hardest-headed man of science. We are only just coming to realize that we can coöperate with and direct this innate force of change which has so long been silently operating, in spite of the respectable lethargy, indifference, and even protests of man himself, the most educable of all its creatures.

At last, perhaps, the long-disputed sin against the Holy Ghost has been found; it may be the refusal to coöperate with the vital principle of betterment. History would seem, in short, to condemn the principle of conservatism as a hopeless and wicked anachronism.

If what has been said above is true, or any considerable part of it, is not almost our whole education at fault? We make no consistent effort to cultivate a progressive spirit in our boys and girls. They are not made to realize the responsibility that rests upon them — the exhilaration that comes from ever looking and pressing forward. They are still so largely nurtured upon the abstract and the classical that we scarcely yet dare to bring education into relation with life. The history they are taught brings few or none of the lessons the past has to offer. They are reared with too much respect for the past, too little confidence for the future. Does not education become in this way a mighty barrier cast across the way of progress, rather than a guidepost to betterment? Would not most of those in charge of the education of our youth tremble before the possibility of having them realize fully what has been hinted in this essay? What would happen if the teachers in our schools and colleges, our theological seminaries and law schools, should make it their business to emphasize the temporary and provisional character of the instruction that they offer, and urge the students to transcend it as fast as a progressive world permitted? The humorous nature of such a suggestion shows how far we are still from any general realization and acceptance of the great lesson of history.

"Let us," to quote Maeterlinck once more, "think of the great invisible ship that carries our human destinies upon eternity. Like the vessels of our confined oceans, she has her sails and her ballast. The fear that she may pitch or roll on leaving the roadstead is no reason for increasing the weight of the ballast by stowing the fair white sails in the depths of the hold. They were not woven to molder side by side with cobblestones in the dark. Ballast exists everywhere; all the pebbles of the harbor, all the sand of the beach, will serve for that. But sails are rare and precious things; their place is not in the murk of the well, but amid the light of the tall masts, where they will collect the winds of space."

DATE DUE